Wilhelm von Lenz

The Great Piano Virtuosos of Our Time

Liszt, Chopin, Tausig, Henselt

Lenz, Wilhelm von

The Great Piano Virtuosos of Our Time
Liszt, Chopin, Tausig, Henselt

ISBN/EAN: 978-3-86741-433-3

First published in 2010 by Europaeischer Hochschulverlag GmbH & Co KG, Bremen, Germany.

© Europaeischer Hochschulverlag GmbH & Co KG, Fahrenheitstr. 1, D-28359 Bremen (www.ehv-online.com). All rights reserved.

Cover: Foto © Christian Seidel/Pixelio

This book is a reproduction of an out of print title and has originally been published by Schirmer , New York (1899). Because no electronic master copies of this title could be obtained, the publisher had to reuse old copies of the text. We therefore apologize for any possible loss in quality.

The Great Piano Virtuosos of Our Time

FROM PERSONAL ACQUAINTANCE

Liszt, Chopin, Tausig, Henselt

BY
W. VON LENZ

Author of "Beethoven et ses trois Styles," and "Beethoven, eine Kunststudie."

TRANSLATED FROM THE GERMAN BY
MADELEINE R. BAKER

NEW YORK
G. Schirmer
MDCCCXCIX

TO THE MEMORY OF
COUNTS MICHAEL AND MATHIAS
WIELHORSKI
MY FATHERLY FRIENDS
AND BENEFACTORS

*VOS, MUSICÆ PRINCIPES,
MORITURUS SALUTAT*

Note

THE first part of the following Recollections of my musical life appeared in 1868 in the "Neue Berliner Musikzeitung." Tausig wished the articles collected and published separately, and corresponded with me on the subject. These essays — to which I have added one on Adolph Henselt — will now have a wider circulation than would be possible through the columns of the "Neue Berliner Musikzeitung."

The Author

Franz Liszt

Majore cultu

Franz Liszt

ALL the great pianists of the first half of the century, were personally known to me: Field, Hummel, Moscheles, Kalkbrenner. From the school which we now already call "old" (excluding Field, who went his own peculiar way), a school which, if not founded by Hummel, was at least essentially influenced by him, I came to the new era of the pianoforte, to Liszt and Chopin.

Liszt is a phenomenon of universal musical virtuosity, such as had *never* before been known: not simply a pianistic wonder. Liszt is a phenomenon spreading over the whole domain of musical production, and creating a universal standard of comparison.

Liszt does not merely *play piano;* he tells, at the piano, the story of his own destiny, which is closely linked to, and reflects, the progress of our time. Liszt is a *latent history* of the keyboard, himself its crowning glory. To him the piano becomes an approximate expression of his high mental cultivation, of his views, of his faith and being. What does *piano-playing* matter to him!—"*Steig' auf*

Great Piano Virtuosos

den Thurm, und siehe wie die Schlacht sich wendet" ["Climb the tower, and see how the battle goes"] —that is what one should say of him; how far inquiry has reached into the domain of science, how far speculation has fathomed musical thought; how it goes in the world of intellect—that is what one has to learn from his playing (how else were such playing possible?), and to learn for the *first* time, for one could never go so far alone.

His wish to become a priest rose from the innermost core of his being. It was *thematic*. The man of the world in Liszt is but an episode from the *theme*. To the priest alone are the portals of infinity the home of the soul. Priest in continuation of Prophet; and Liszt was ever a prophet from the beginning of his career.

When Liszt thunders, lightens, sighs on the piano that "Song of Songs"—the great *B flat major Sonata* for *Hammerklavier*—by Beethoven, he coins capital for mankind out of the ideas of the greatest musical thinker the world has ever known, who could have had no conception of *such* a rendering of his *Hammerklavier* music; he wrote his later piano-music (from Op. 100 on) for the transcendence (viewed through the spectroscope of his

Franz Liszt

orchestral conceptions at the piano) of his *musical* thought, not of his *piano*-thought.

The pianist in Liszt is an apparition [Gespenst], not to be compressed within the bounds of the house drawn by schools and professors!

The old proverb applies here: "Quod licet *Jovi*, non licet *bovi!*"

Nothing could be more foolish than to attempt to *imitate* Liszt, or even to use *him* as a measure by which to criticise others. Where Liszt appears, all other pianists disappear; there remains only the *piano*, and that trembles in its whole body!

Liszt is the past, the present, and the future of the piano; how, then, should he find time to be a *professor* and pattern besides? He is the spirit of the matter; he absorbs the conception. How can that which is perishable hope to vie with the imperishable?—This entire pianistic stronghold is the material side of the matter; it was never the spirit of the matter, however much spirit may have occupied the guest-chamber. One cannot suspend a ghost as a barometer in the sitting-room! So Liszt is no pattern, only the beginning, continuation, and end! Hence, in Liszt's case, any comparison of any given performance at the piano is

Great Piano Virtuosos

a priori out of the question; because he is the exception, because he is the prophet who has ceased to be a plain citizen, in order to become a soldier of the spirit in *his own* church, *his own* ideas. Such a brain must be rated higher than a piano, and it is an accidental circumstance, of no importance, that Liszt plays the piano at all. Perhaps, in a higher sense *(majore cultu)*, this is in fact not the case, the piano being merely visible, like the *tub* in Mesmer's case! It is wholly uncritical to say that *Liszt* does *this* or *that* differently from some one else; do not imagine that Liszt *does* anything—he *does* nothing at all; he *thinks*, and *what* he thinks takes on this form. That is the process. Can this be called *piano-playing?* "Thee now the body leaveth, and God the soul receiveth,"[1] for now everything leads upward, onward,—excelsior!

Liszt, then, cannot be expected to practise scales and finger-exercises, as is the custom among schools and professors!—Does the eagle practise flying? he looks upwards, gazes towards the sun, unfolds his pinions, and soars towards its burning light!

Such is the relation of Liszt to the piano, and it is not given to every one to follow his flight,

Franz Liszt

thereby forgetting the unhappy instrument, the starting-point!

I will relate the circumstances which brought me to Liszt, as one makes the acquaintance of *such* a spirit in no ordinary way; one gains access to him, or one does not. That is the whole matter, and signifies much in either case.

In 1828 (forty-three years ago!) I was nineteen years old, and had come to Paris to pursue my studies *(humaniores litteræ)* on a broader scale, above all to continue my work in French channels, and to take piano-lessons (as people used to say), but with Kalkbrenner. Kalkbrenner was a native of Berlin, of Jewish extraction; in Paris he was the *Joconde* of the *salon*-piano, under Charles the Tenth. He was a knight of the Legion of Honor, and farmer-general of all permissible pianistic elegancies. The beautiful Camille Mock, later Mme. Pleyel—to whose charms neither Liszt nor Chopin was indifferent—was the favorite pupil of the irresistible Kalkbrenner. I heard her play from the manuscript, with Kalkbrenner and Onslow, the latter's *sextuor*. It was at the home of Baron Trémont, a tame musical Mæcenas of the time, in Paris. She played the piano as one wears an elegant shoe,

Great Piano Virtuosos

when one is a pretty Parisian. Nevertheless, I was in danger of becoming Kalkbrenner's pupil, but Liszt and my good star ordered it otherwise. On the way to Kalkbrenner (who plays a note of his, nowadays?), as I was walking along the boulevards, I read among the theatre-posters of the day, which exercised so powerful an attraction, the notice of an *extra* concert (it was already November) to be given at the Conservatoire by Mr. Liszt, with Beethoven's *E flat major Piano Concerto* heading the programme.

Beethoven was then (and not only in Paris) Paracelsus personified, in the concert-room. Of Beethoven, at that time, I knew only that I had been frightened by his ladder-like notes in the *D major Trio*, and in the *Fantasia* with chorus, which I had once opened (and at once closed) in a music-store in my native city, Riga, where more was doing in trade than in music.

How astonished I should have been if some one had told me—as I innocently stood before the advertising-column in Paris, and learned from the notice that there were such things as piano-concertos by Beethoven—that some time in the future I should write six volumes in German, and

Franz Liszt

two in French, about Beethoven! I had heard of the *septuor*. In those days Beethoven was called *J. N. Hummel!*

From the concert-notice, I concluded that any one who could publicly play a Beethoven piano-concerto must be a remarkable person, and of quite a different growth from Kalkbrenner, the composer of the Fantasia *Effusio Musica*. That this *Effusio* was a trumpery piece, so much I already understood, young and happy though I was.

It was in this manner—on the fateful Paris boulevards—that I first saw the name of Liszt, which was to fill the world;—on the boulevards where one fancies one is contributing one's part to the daily history of Europe when one takes a walk!

That concert-notice was destined to have a lasting influence on my life. I can still see, after the lapse of so many years, the color of the fateful paper; gigantic black letters on a bright yellow ground (*la couleur distinguée* of those days, in Paris).

I drove straight to Schlesinger, whose place was at that time the musical exchange of Paris, in the Rue Richelieu.

"Where does Mr. Liszt live?" I demanded, and pronounced it *Litz*, for the Parisians never got any

Great Piano Virtuosos

further with *Liszt* than *Litz*. That good German, Rudolf Kreutzer, who chanced at one time to be their best violin-virtuoso, they called *Kretch*, wherefore the man to whom Beethoven dedicated his great violin-sonata, Op. 47, had his cards engraved thus: *Rodolph Kreutzer, prononcez Bertrand*. The Parisians understood that; Parisians are, after all, very "so," as *Falstaff* says.

Liszt's address was Rue Montholon, far away, where Paris imagines that she can become a mountain! What has *not* Paris imagined—and what have we ever refused to believe of her? Mountain and valley, Heaven and Hell—all these has she imagined herself to be!

They gave me Liszt's address at Schlesinger's without any hesitation, but when I asked Litz's price, and made known my wish to study with Litz, they all laughed at me, and the clerks behind the desk giggled with them, and they all said at once: "*He* has never given a lesson, *he* is no *piano-teacher!*"

I felt that I must have said something very stupid! But the reply: "*no piano-teacher*," pleased me, nevertheless, and I made my way at once to Rue Montholon.

Liszt was at home. That was a very unusual thing,

Franz Liszt

his mother told me—an excellent woman with a German heart, who pleased me extremely,—her Franz was almost always at church, she said, and—above all things—*busied himself no more with music!* Those were the days when Liszt wished to become a Saint Simonist; when Père Enfantin infested Paris; when Lamennais wrote the *Paroles d'un Croyant*, and the *Peau de chagrin* of Balzac followed close upon his *Scènes de la vie privée*.

It was a grand epoch, and Paris the navel of the earth. Rossini lived there, and Cherubini, also Auber, Halévy, Berlioz, and the great violinist Baillot; Victor Hugo, who was afterwards banished for political reasons, had published his *Orientales*, and Lamartine was just recovering from the exertion of his *Méditations poétiques*. We should soon be in the midst of the July revolution, but we were still under the Martignac ministry.

Odilon-Barrot spoke *con sordini* in the Chamber, Cuvier lectured in the Jardin des Plantes, Guizot and Villemain in the Sorbonne; Cousin had discovered German philosophy; Lerminier—Savigny and Ganz—one ran from one to the other! Scribe was doing his turn at the theatre, where Mlle. Mars was still playing. Dumas had, after the German style, given his first and best piece, *Henry III et la Cour*, to the Théâtre Français, where the first performance was repressed by the ministry, because there was something in it about "Lilies." Paris piqued herself upon possessing both the Classic and the Romantic Schools, and these factions were at swords' points. During the reign of Charles X., there were masked balls at court, at which the Duchesse de Berry appeared as Maria Stuart, the Duc de Chartres as Francis I.; the Duchesse de Berry's lovely foot was much talked of, and Salvandy said—at the Duc d'Orléans' ball in the Palais Royal—"We are dancing on a volcano." George Sand was not yet well known—Chopin not yet in Paris. Marie Taglioni danced at the Grand Opéra, Habenek, a German master, conducted the Élite Orchestra at the Conservatoire—where the Parisians, one year after Beethoven's death, heard, for the first time, some of his music. Malibran and Sontag sang the "tourney" duet in *Tancredi* at the Italian Opera. It was the winter of 1828–1829; Baillot played in quartets, and Rossini gave his *Tell* early in the New Year.

In Liszt I found a pale, haggard young man, with unspeakably attractive features. He was reclining

Franz Liszt

on a broad sofa, apparently lost in deep reflection, and smoking a long Turkish pipe. Three pianos stood near. He did not make the slightest motion when I entered—did not even seem to notice me.

When I explained to him, in French—at that time no one presumed to address him in any other language—that my family had sent me to Kalkbrenner, but that I came to him because he dared to play a Beethoven *Concerto* in public—he seemed to smile; it was, however, like the glitter of a dagger in the sunlight.

"Play me something," said he, with indescribable sarcasm, which, nevertheless, did not hurt my feelings—any more, for instance, than one feels insulted when it thunders.

"I will play the *Kalkbrenner Sonata* for the left hand," said I, feeling that I had chosen well.

"*That* I will not hear, I do not know it, and I do not care to know it!" he answered, with yet stronger sarcasm and scarcely concealed scorn.

I felt that I was playing a pitiable rôle—perhaps I was expiating the sins of some one else, of some Parisian. However, I said to myself, as I looked at this young Parisian—for in appearance he was thoroughly Parisian—that he must surely be a genius;

Great Piano Virtuosos

and thus, without further skirmishing, I did not care to be driven from the field by any Parisian.

With modest, but firm step I approached the nearest piano.

"Not that one!" cried Liszt, without in the least changing his half-recumbent position on the sofa, "there, at the other one!"

I walked to the second piano. At that time I was absorbed in the *Invitation to the Dance*; I had married it out of pure love, two years before, and we were still in our honeymoon. I came from Riga, where the unexampled success of *Der Freischütz*[2] had prepared the way for Weber's piano compositions, while in Paris *Der Freischütz* was called *Robin (!) des bois*, and was *embellished* by Berlioz with recitative!

I had studied with good masters. When I tried to strike the three first A flats I found it quite impossible to make the instrument give forth a sound—what was the matter? I struck *hard;* the A flat sounded, but quite *piano*. I appeared very foolish, I felt sure of that, but without losing courage I went bravely on to the entrance of the first chord—then Liszt got up, came over to me, pulled my right hand off the keyboard and asked: "What is *that?* That begins well!

Franz Liszt

"I should think it did," I answered, with the pride of a parish clerk for his pastor, "that is by Weber!"
"Has he written for the piano, too?" he asked, astounded. "Here, we only know his *Robin des bois!*"
"Certainly he has written for the piano, and more beautifully than any one else," was my equally surprised answer. "I carry in my trunk," I continued, "two Polonaises, two Rondos, four Variation-Numbers,[3] four Sonatas; one of the Sonatas, which I studied with Vehrstaedt in Geneva, contains the whole of Switzerland, and is inexpressibly beautiful—in it all lovely women smile at once—it is in A flat major—you can't imagine how beautiful it is, no one has written anything to compare with it for the piano, believe me."

I spoke from my heart, and so convincingly that Liszt was strongly impressed.

Presently he said in his most winning tone: "Please bring me everything you have in your trunk, and, *for the first time in my life*, I will give lessons—to *you*—because you have introduced me to Weber's piano-music, and because you did not allow yourself to be discouraged by the hard action of this piano. I ordered it myself; *one* scale played on such a piano is equal to *ten* on any other; it is a completely *im-*

Great Piano Virtuosos

possible piano. It was a *mauvaise plaisanterie* on my part—but *why* did you speak of Kalkbrenner and his Sonata for the left hand? But now, play me your piece *('votre chose')* that begins so curiously. That piano you first tried is one of the finest instruments in Paris."

Then I played, most enthusiastically, the *Invitation*, but only the *Cantilena*, marked *wiegend* (swaying, rocking), in two parts. Liszt was charmed with the composition. "You must bring me that," said he, "we will interpret it to each other!"

Thus the last letter of the alphabet came to the first.

In our first lesson, Liszt could scarcely tear himself away from the piece. He played through the different parts again and again; tried various reinforcements; played the second part of the minor movement in octaves, and was inexhaustible in his praise of Weber. And what, indeed, did one find at that time in the piano-repertory? The bland masterjoiner *Hummel; Herz; Kalkbrenner*, and *Moscheles;* nothing plastic, dramatic, or speaking, for the piano; Beethoven was not yet understood; of his thirty-two Sonatas, *three were* played (!)—the *A flat major Sonata* with the variations (Op. 26), the

Franz Liszt

C sharp minor quasi Fantasia, and the *Sonata in F minor*, which a publisher's fancy—not Beethoven—christened *appassionata*. The five last ones passed for the monstrous abortions of a German idealist who did not know how to write for piano. People understood only Hummel and Co.; Mozart was too old-fashioned, and did not write such passages as Herz, Kalkbrenner, Moscheles,—to say nothing of the lesser lights.

In the midst of this "Flowery Kingdom" dwelt Liszt, and one must take this into account, in order to grasp the greatness of the man who discovered Weber and his own genius at the piano, when he was but twenty years old!

Liszt was wholly enraptured with Weber's *A flat major Sonata*. I had studied it in Geneva, with Vehrstaedt,[4] and expressed in my rendering the true spirit of the composition. Liszt proved this to me by the way he listened, by his gestures, by his exclamations of approval. We were as one man, in our admiration for Weber.

This great romantic poem for the piano begins with a tremolo in the bass, on A flat. No Sonata ever began that way, before! It is like the sunrise over an enchanted forest wherein the action takes place!

Great Piano Virtuosos

The uneasiness of my master over the first part of the First Allegro became so great that, before I came to the close, he shoved me aside, saying: "Wait—wait! what is that? I must play that myself!"—I had never before heard anything like that! Think of a genius like Liszt, but twenty years old, coming into contact, for the first time, with such a capital composition—with the apparition of that Knight in Golden Armor, Weber!

He tried the first part over and over again in various ways; at the passage (in the dominant) in E flat at the close of the first part, he said: "It is marked *ligato* there, would it not be better to make it *pp. staccato (piqué)*? *Leggermente* is prescribed there, too." He experimented in every direction.

So I had the privilege of observing how *one* genius looks upon the work of another and turns it to his own account! So we learned some special lesson every day, from our two hours' sojourn with Weber!

"Now, how is the second part of the first Allegro?" asked Liszt, as he examined it. It seemed to me quite impossible that any one could read at sight this part through which the theme is carried in crowded octaves several pages long!

"That is very hard," said Liszt, "and the Coda is

Franz Liszt

still harder; to hold the whole together in this centrifugal figure near the end (thirteen measures before the close) is very difficult. This passage (in the second part—of course in the principal key, A flat) we will not play *staccato*, that would be somewhat affected *(recherché)*; neither will we make it *ligato*, that is too thin; we will make it *spiccato*; let us swim between the two waters" *(nageons entre les deux eaux!)*.

If I admired the fire and life, the spiritual passion in Liszt's production of the first part—in the second part I was astounded by his confident repose and certainty, the way in which he held himself back in order to reserve his strength for the last attack!

So young and so wise! I said to myself; I felt disheartened and discouraged.

I learned more from Liszt in the first four measures of the Andante of that Sonata, than I had gotten in years, from my earlier masters.

"This exposition is to be after the manner of Baillot when he plays in quartet, the accompanying parts are in the lifted sixteenth-notes; but Baillot's parts are very good, you must not make them inferior to his. You have a *good* hand, you *can* learn it; look sharp, it is not easy—one can move stones with that; I can imagine how the piano-hussars chase through that! I shall never forget that I became acquainted with that Sonata through *you*. Well, you shall learn something from me; I will tell you everything I know about our instrument."

The thirty-second-note figure in the bass of the Andante (thirty-fifth measure) one too often hears played as a *passage* for the left hand; the figure should be expressed *caressingly*, it should be a violoncello solo *amoroso!* So Liszt played it; but lent terrible majesty to the octave-irruption upon the second theme in C, which Henselt calls the "Ten Commandments"—a capital title.

How can I begin to express what Liszt did with the Menuetto capriccioso and Rondo of the Sonata, the very first time he saw these inspired compositions? What was there *not* in his treatment of the clarinet solo in the trio of the Menuetto, the modulation of that cry of longing, the winding ornamentation of the Rondo!

After considering the composer's manner of handling the piano, and of writing for it, one may confidently say of the Weber sonatas that—as an expression of the Instrument, as specific piano-music— they leave the Beethoven sonatas behind (*not* as *musical* ideas for which the piano is the medium of expression). The Mozart sonatas are cartoons for quartets, the Beethoven sonatas, symphonic rhapsodies; but the noble Weber sonatas—as such—are the happiest expression of the piano, in its most happy mood. The piano of Weber is quite innocent of quartet or symphony; it is self-dependent, self-sufficient, conscious *piano*, and opened the door to the New School, to the treatment of the instrument by Liszt and Chopin.

And has there ever been manifested greater genius in the handling of the piano, than is found in Weber's *first* Sonata—the one in C major?

One is astounded at this work of the year 1813 (in which it was criticized by that great blindwoman, the *Allgemeine musikalische Zeitung*), a work which may have been composed still earlier,—that had emancipated itself in such a degree from the forms controlling musical thought sixty years (!) ago, and from all social and socio-political relations and conditions in life! For in Art we do not part the spirit from the form. The paternal home, the hearth, the household altar, the *häusliche Jahreszeit*, are the *motives* of the Weber *Sonata in C;* the youthful soul thus finds expression for its impulse towards the unknown country which lies behind the narrow precincts of his homely native town! This longing supplied Weber with words for his sonata-poem in C, a second *Glocke*.

Vom Mädchen reisst sich stolz der Knabe! —

is the clear meaning of the diminished chord at the beginning, through which Weber's poem rushes into life.

The Weber sonatas unite us to life; Beethoven's relation to life—at the piano—is that of the preacher to the parish.

Of Liszt's magnificent interpretation of Weber, of the Alexandrian triumphal processions he made throughout Europe with Weber's piano-compositions—especially his *Concertstück*—the world knows, and future generations will talk about it.

I now come to a thought, respected Reader, which I fancy is original, because no one else has spoken it, and because it explains Liszt's wonderful manner of writing for the piano as arising from esoteric causes, and gives to his mechanical difficulties an externally artificial appearance.

I understand Liszt's manner of writing for piano as a satire on the distinctions of rank, the conventionalities and absurdities of the early Parisian *salons*, which, in their pitiful puerility, through three different forms of Parisian government, I had opportunity to note. These weak pretensions of every sort, constituted in those days the difference between France and Germany, and between France and the freer atmosphere of St. Petersburg, where the Artist, as the epitome of culture, is equal in rank to the highest-born of the land; there, the relation of the artist to the world about him, turns rather in the opposite extreme, and this condition of affairs is not always conducive to his own happiness.

The difficulties of Liszt's style are—so to speak— variations upon his own Parisian theme: "*Stirb, Vogel, oder friss!*"[5]

Liszt tossed these technical difficulties in the faces of the Parisians:—"I require no thanks, ladies," says he; "do this after me," says he, "*who* and *what* are you?" he asks. He who did not live in Paris, was not to be considered as living at all. Of this city Liszt was at once the scourge and the darling. His method, hard to describe, is an expression of his native, unparalleled pianistic technique, and it would be a great mistake to imagine that any one could ever approach such individuality, no matter how thoroughly he might overcome the difficulties of his piano-mechanism. It has been said: "Let all composers assemble, and let each instrument the simple chord of C major; Beethoven's chord would be Beethoven!" *That* is the kernel of the whole matter! It is not otherwise with Liszt; let all the pianists come together and attack the *E flat major Piano Concerto* by Beethoven (to take this as an example); Liszt's first stroke will betray the fact that it is he and no other! His phantasy (imagination) is imponderable; it is disembodied; all other pianists are lost in the shadow cast by Liszt; he is a doctor like *Faust*, and *we* are his *Wagner!*

The friendly reader of these leaves of remembrance, has *not* my permission, after noting our criticism of others, to ask: But *Liszt?*

That is just my point: "That is the humour of it," says Pistol; that was our meaning—Liszt is an apparition!

Since one has to go to Rome in order to *see* Liszt— to say nothing at all about *hearing* him;—ever since Liszt turned his back upon the public, one has only the right to speak of *having heard* him, and must no longer call him a *pianist*—Liszt may be likened to a dead man, who fortunately is still alive—a pianist he is not. In his personality, he is

Franz Liszt

an image of our day, in which more happens than formerly took place in centuries; apart from his musical hegemony,[6] Liszt is one of the great intellects of the century.

As for the explanation and proper view of Liszt's particular manner of writing; of himself, of his favored nature, I may say: Art is the ideal Truth of earthly life, she is the disembodied Truth. She can exhibit herself in diverse ways. The difficulties in Liszt are nothing external—they are a key to his inmost being. Were these difficulties but outwardly represented—as one but too often experiences— they would remain something outward and superficial—the clod would cling to them, and the spirit would remain with the composer.

Chopin

> *Il ne faut pas s'en nourrir,
> mais s'en servir comme
> d'une essence.* — P<small>ASCAL</small>

Chopin

EUROPE, from Madrid to St. Petersburg, was lionizing Liszt, when, in 1842, we again found ourselves in Paris, where Louis Philippe had become King. Twelve years had elapsed since the year 1830, when the French nation hung upon the word of the Citizen King; it was, nevertheless, a great and stirring time, a time of ideas, and Paris, through the influence she exercised on manners and customs—but still more through the belief, universally shared, in her dictatorial supremacy—was the central Sun in the constellation of Europe.

Life had become elegantly frivolous; under Charles X. it had been simply corrupt. Then, Vice had worn its livery; now it was transformed into a *demi-monde*, with all sorts of socially authorized titles, with the accepted grades of "Duchesse," "Camélia," etc. "Grisettes" were promoted to "Lorettes"—a cognomen which, if I'm not mistaken, originated with Thiers, or some great politician of the time,[7] and was suggested by that pretty church, Notre Dame de Lorette, in whose neighborhood, in the *beau quartier* of the city, this fraction of urban society was wont to dwell. At that time Thiers lived in the parish of the church of Notre Dame de Lorette, Place St.-George, in the pleasant hôtel of his mother-in-law, Madame Deaune, with a small garden next the street. He was, from time to time, minister to King Louis Philippe—which did not amount to much, and never lasted long. Thiers certainly did not then believe that a Revolution would find it worth while to raze his house to the ground, or that he, the little Advocate from Marseilles, was destined to rise on the *ruins*, as President of the French Republic! *Impavidum ferient ruinæ!*

At that time—1842—George Sand was an established fact. The whole range of Camélia literature was in full bloom; Balzac thought that Paris breathed an electric atmosphere; Paris was a *milieu*, in which alone one could live.

In this *milieu* lived Chopin. Just now, however—in the month of August—he was still in Touraine with George Sand, living in a château of too diminutive proportions to be designated as a "castle." In truth, the spirit of this time, and of the Pleiades of Art and Literature which it produced, was manifested in wishing to *appear* greater than one *was*, and to *spend* what one did not have at all! The term "dis-

Chopin

tinguished" *(le distingué)* took the lead, and went through the most kaleidoscopic gradations. To return to Paris before the month of November; above all, if one shut one's self up in Paris through the summer, was *not* "distinguished"! And Chopin was *very* distinguished—not like dead-and-gone Kalkbrenner, as a peacock, or a silver pheasant (neither was he decorated with the smallest Legion of Honor ribbon), but as a *great artist*, although a good, fashionable Parisian, was Chopin distinguished. In his easy, well-bred reserve, in his manners, in his whole outward appearance, he sought to be, and was, distinguished.

This time I came from St. Petersburg to Paris, not from Riga, by way of Geneva. Since the *A flat major Weber Sonata*, I had passed fourteen years in St. Petersburg, *quantum mutatus ab illo!* Liszt was in Paris, fresh from his unexampled St. Petersburg triumph, where he—before four thousand people, alone, and without accompaniment—appeared in the Hall of the Nobility; where women of the highest rank awaited him on the steps of his hotel, with garlands of flowers; where the greatest nobles secured a steamboat, with choruses of singers, in order fittingly to accompany the great artist as far

Great Piano Virtuosos

as Kronstadt, and further—to the roadstead of the Gulf of Finland, when he sailed for Germany.

My first visit in Paris was to Liszt, who lived in Rue Blanche, not far from our Rue Montholon of 1828. The mother of the great artist again received me most kindly, but she did not tell me, as formerly, that I "wearied her Franz," he was always "in a dreadful way" after I, with my Weber Sonatas, had been to see him! Her son did not attend church so assiduously, he carried his church about in himself, and no longer desired to become a St. Simonist.

Liszt himself received me right royally. His first words were: "I shall go to see you every day; you live so conveniently near Schlesinger, where I go so often; I shall send you an Érard grand, and, at the instrument, we will live over again the good old times, especially the Weber Sonatas; I suppose you have them with you?"

"In the same copy, with your notes, which I keep as a holy relic—but I should like some Chopin."

"We will study whatever you like, only don't dare imagine that you are to pay me—for no price would I give lessons. I shall visit a friend; all I ask is a cup of coffee from the hotel. I will come every day

Chopin

promptly at two o'clock, and we will agree upon afternoon and evening, as you must spend the entire morning at the piano—I shall send you the very best, I shall go myself to Érard's and select one."

Those were afternoons never to be forgotten! Liszt seldom missed the hour—another mark of his unfailing politeness. I see him standing in the doorway of my hotel, his hat on his head, an elegant Verdier stick in his hand, his spiritual, speaking countenance laughing up at me! It made me feel as though *I* had been made king in Paris!

Once I played his own arrangement of Schubert's *Ständchen* to him.

"Give me a pencil," said he, and wrote in it: *Comme naturaliste, parfait,* with *Franz Liszt,* in his crooked signature.

"How *naturaliste?*" I objected, "when I have had *you* for a teacher?"

"Well; you play it very well; heartily, very heartily, and quite faultlessly, but *not* like a virtuoso; and only such an one—and how few among *them* —can play the Coda as I wish; it is *diablement* hard, not in the reading, but as a whole, and in virtuoso-like expression. That is what I mean."

Great Piano Virtuosos

We next came to Weber's *Polacca in E major*.
"There is more virtuoso work," said he; "you play it very well, but you have not sufficient strength, one must be possessed of a devil to play that."

I played the *Moonlight Trio*.

"You play that *well*," said Liszt, animatedly, "look you, that is perfect—give me the pencil;" and he wrote in it: *Ceci est parfait*—"do you see, this is the antidote for the Schubert! Where did you learn that fingering? that change from the thumb to the second finger, and back again [in the dotted middle part on *b* and *e*]? That is not your own invention; it is good, but somewhat choppy, one might come to a standstill—whose is that fingering?"

"It is by Moscheles in London; in the time *after* you—1829!"

"Oh! ho! was *he* so learned in Weber? Now, *I* will play the Polacca to *you*, it will be better."

I always went as far as the court-yard with him, and as he went down the winding stairs he repeated several times: "That *Trio* was capital—capital! You had not practised it, had you? It is very difficult in this *cantilena*; one does not get that from one's so-called *strong* pupils—here in

Chopin

Paris, *never*. So, keep to Weber, there is your native soil!"

Then I *was* happy, and began to consider myself a *foudre de guerre* at the piano! How happy conceit can make one! Those were blessed days, those days of the Weber alliance with Liszt!

Since then Liszt has been happily inspired to unite the serious, striking *Introduction* of Weber's first (insignificant) *Polacca in E flat* to the second *Polacca in E*, that noble ancestress of the species,— to arrange the whole for piano and orchestra, and so to honor the bravura repertory with an inestimable gift. The connecting part between the Weber *Introduction* and the Weber *Polacca*, composed by Liszt, is the most tasteful and intelligent piece of work one can imagine; it is like a beautiful face whose expression reveals the soul of romance! It is like the enchanted wood of Titania in the midst of other forests! It is inimitably conceived! *Chopin* would have wept over it! *He* never soared so high! He never rose to the romantic, he remained poetically material. He sat, a prisoner in the glitter of the conventional atmosphere of Paris, in its most becoming toilette of conventional tenets!

Great Piano Virtuosos

One morning Liszt said: "It is fine weather, let us go for a walk—but, what have you there for a great-coat?"

"A sort of tigerskin of brown velvet; I got it in Hamburg; it fits snug, and suits me."

"That will make you conspicuous in Paris! *I* am the *only* man in Paris who can afford to give you his arm, while you wear that Hanseatic pelt; come on. We will get some macaroni at Broschi's, opposite the Grand Opera: Rossini goes there—we will sit at his table."

As we walked along the Boulevards, and I noticed how curiously the people looked after us, I understood Liszt's remark—that *he* alone might dare to show himself with any one wearing such a garment. Chopin would never have done it, it might have displeased the Sand! So strange, so affected, so *small* was—and ever will be—the great city of Paris!

The Weber *A flat major Sonata* came *post tot errores*, in its turn. "Very good, very good," said Liszt, to the Rondo among other things—"but still too little of the little Countess B—— in St. Petersburg: the eloquent foot is wanting." He played the foot. I studied, and went through the

Chopin

Rondo again under his hawk-eyes. "Now it is right," said he, "the foot is there, but where is the shoe?" He played the *shoe*. Thus he always had to say and do something, and he was always right. It was the passage in the Rondo (twenty-fourth and following measures) with the serpentine scales in the bass in F minor. Liszt forgot it long ago, in Rome. I shall remember it.

In Chopin's *B flat major* and *A minor Mazurkas*, Op. 7, I learned much about piano-playing in general from Liszt. In both pieces he noted important little variants, taking the matter very seriously, especially the apparently so easy bass in the *Maggiore* of the *A minor Mazurka*. What pains he took with me there! "Only an ass could think *that* was easy," said he; "in these slurrings one recognizes the virtuoso! Play it thus to Chopin, and he will notice something; it will please him. These stupid French editions bungle everything of his; these slurs must run *so* in the bass!"

"If you play that *so* to *him* he will give you lessons, only you must summon the courage to do it," concluded Liszt.

It was already October, and Chopin still so *distingué* that he was not in Paris. With the most amiable

Great Piano Virtuosos

sympathy Liszt said to me one morning: "Now he is coming, I feel sure of it, if the Sand will only let him go!" I said: "If he would only let *Indiana* go!"

"That he will not do," Liszt replied, "I know that. When he is here, I will bring him directly to you; after all, *you* have the Érard; and we shall play, as if by chance, the Onslow four-hand *Sonata in F minor* that you are so fond of; we have already played it once in Paris—in public; curiously enough Chopin played the primo,—that was my idea, and he'll be glad to do it again. You must have the Sonata; get it at Schlesinger's, and try to secure the Leipzig edition—that is correct. In this way you will most easily get lessons from him, it will arrange itself—particularly now, in the beginning of the season. You can't imagine how difficult it is, because you don't know Paris yet. With me, for example, it is nothing, but hard, *so hard* with Chopin! How many have journeyed all the way to Paris, and have not been able even to get a glimpse of him!"

From the time I dared hope to hear Liszt and Chopin play in *my* apartments, I walked on air in Paris; I was greeted in front of the music-shops; they offered me a chair every time I went into

Chopin

Schlesinger's—I had passed there with Liszt! At Schlesinger's I met Berlioz; he understood little of piano-music, and looked—in his blue frock-coat with brass buttons, and decorated with the well-earned Legion of Honor—like a musical Robert Macaire; a character whom Frédéric Lemaître successfully exhibited at the Theatre of the Porte St-Martin. Berlioz called Liszt *le cher sublime*, which was considered very *spirituel*—people, in those times, were regularly astonished if any one dared to clamber over the hedge of speech.

When I again met Berlioz, in St. Petersburg in 1868, after the loss of his only son, his hope and his joy, he looked like the Vicar of Wakefield at a funeral; it was no use, then, to speak to him of Liszt; he had come to consider the *B flat major Symphony* of Beethoven the most beautiful of all! There lay the poor, suffering man (always on his back) in the palace of the Grand-duchess Helena, where he lived. There, at his bedside, I read to him my report of the concert directed by him, and given, under the patronage of the Grand-duchess, by the Russian Musical Society; and there he gave me, at parting, his daguerreotype with this inscription in his own hand: *À l'homme qui a sû aimer et*

Great Piano Virtuosos

admirer!! Son frère dévoué, Hector Berlioz. Berlioz was unhappier than King Lear!

October was here, but still no Chopin! With trouble and some sacrifices, I obtained an extension of my leave of absence from St. Petersburg, waited patiently, and was as diligent as possible at my Érard. I well remember how, in that cabriolet which I mounted at the risk of my neck, in order to traverse the famous *milieu* "with the electrical atmosphere" in all directions, and learn it thoroughly, I used continually to practise—on the wooden *apron* enclosing the seat—the *volate* that Liszt had noted for me in the Chopin *B flat major Mazurka*—so as to "keep my right hand in." The particular point was this,—instead of returning to the theme, from f to f (an octave lower), to go two octaves higher, and then fall back into the lower octave,—that is, to take twelve f's in triplets, and by no chance to miss coming in on time! Under Liszt's hands, this was a rocket with its returning shower of stars, in the reprise of the theme!

I mention this in order to warn adepts *never* to presume to attempt anything like it. These naïve mistakes always mislead, and make one appear as

Chopin

ridiculous as is a German who *tries* to speak French—to quote Goethe.

One evening Liszt came to see me with the excellent pianist, Hiller, and the well-known violin-virtuoso, Ernst. The good piano was at *my* lodgings, and plenty of music at hand. Liszt played with Hiller the overture to *Der Freischütz*, and Ernst fiddled with them with might and main. The idea had come into these gentlemen's heads that noon, and Ernst had brought his violin along. It was a remarkable performance. They remained for the evening, and "made jokes of all kinds," as Liszt expressed it. "Where does Cramer live?" I asked. "He has founded a Lancaster Pianoforte School," replied Liszt; "you cannot see him, he is never in the city—he lives in the suburb of Batignolles!"

Cramer, who had become a millionaire in London, speculated through a banker, and lost everything. He became an Englishman in England, and had now come to Paris, which did not suit him. "Cramer is a septuagenarian, leave him alone," concluded Liszt; "from him you can learn nothing, since you have *me*."

I did not leave Cramer alone; to me he was sanctified, *venerabilis Beda!* I had heard him at a concert

Great Piano Virtuosos

at the Argyle Rooms, in London, in 1829; he played capitally—the *Piano-quartet in E flat* by Mozart—with Lindley, the English violoncellist; and Franz Cramer, brother of Jean Baptiste, played the violin. In memory of this, I wrote Cramer a respectful note; Count Wielhorsky had met him in Rome, and had told me much about him. That was the connecting-link. The author of the world-renowned *Études*—that hymn-book of unconfirmed pianists—Church-Father Cramer, answered me, and promised to come. "Now," I said to myself, "order an English dinner—all the dishes served at one time, the best port wine, and *all his works* upon the table!" *His complete works*, a huge pile of music sent from Schlesinger's, must have been covered with a layer of dust a finger thick—but they were in good condition. They contained the history of a whole human life!

I drove about an entire day in order to procure a first-class English meal and port wine. Such a singular place is Paris; conscious only of itself.

Unfortunately Liszt had already left Paris. He would not have refused to play Church-Father Cramer from the pile! That would have been an event, indeed!

Chopin

Cramer appeared on the stroke of seven—he had written me that he would not be out of *school* any earlier! I could hardly believe my eyes! From my youth up, Cramer had stood in a holy shrine at Riga, and here he stood bodily before me! I kissed his hand heartily. He was embarrassed, but it had seemed to me the proper thing to do. "I have but this to offer you," said I, and led him to the tower of his assembled works.

"Are *all* those mine?" he sighed; "have I written all that? Who is acquainted with it now? But I am glad, I am *very* glad"—he shook my hand in English fashion. We spoke French; English seemed out of place to me, unless Cramer had begun; and German is not a language fitted to Paris; Parisian penetrates into every nook and cranny of life, there!

Dinner was served. Everything *English*, even plates and glasses; he noticed it at once. "Do you live in English fashion?" he demanded. "It is a little attention to you!" I replied. That seemed to please him. "There was a time when I drank such wine," said he, as he tasted the port, "but where did you find it here? *Aux Trois Têtes de Mores*, that is said to be the only place where one can find good porto, in Paris. Some one told me of it, it is an American firm—strange city, this Paris, is it not? I do not like it, I should have done better, had I gone to Germany, but the climate here agrees with me; I have already been here some years, and am too old now to go further."

Cramer was sparing of words and answered always quietly and deliberately—*moderato*. When I asked him about Chopin, he said: "I do not understand him, but he plays beautifully and correctly, oh! very correctly; he does not allow himself to become careless, like other young people, but I do not understand him; Liszt is a phenomenon, neither does *he* always play his own compositions. I do not understand this modern music."

The atmosphere at table was depressing—why? Cramer seemed to me to cling too closely to the past, for the present to have any interest for him. I, sitting opposite to him, seemed so insignificant and young—with my thirty-three years! After dinner, however, Cramer became more talkative; I made a diversion with the Érard, and asked him to allow me to play to him his first three studies. He sat down by me, in the friendliest manner—and so I took, *de facto*, lessons of J. B. Cramer!

Chopin

I should never have allowed myself to dream of such a thing in my young days! Vehrstaedt of Geneva played the *Études* as repertory-music; with him I had studied the third in D major, with the intricate fingering, all carefully slurred, with a full *cantilena*, as a prayer, as a slumber-song—what you will. Cramer said: "From me you have nothing to learn. Those are exercises; do you play such things for *pleasure?*"

"Indeed I do!" I opened the *Étude in F* with the triplet-figure in eighth-notes. "See here! What a pastoral!" I spoke of Henselt in St. Petersburg, who played the *Étude* so wonderfully. It seemed to please him.

At my request, Cramer played the first three *Études*. It was dry, wooden, harsh; with no *cantilena* in the third one, in D major, but rounded and masterly. The impression I received was painful, extremely painful! Was *that* Cramer? Had the great man lived so long, only to remain so far behind the times? I did my best to prevent the appearance of any sign of my disillusion; I had, however, entirely lost my bearings, and did not know what to say! I asked him if he did not think an *absolutes Ligato* indicated in this third *Étude?* He had cut short

Great Piano Virtuosos

off the notes in the upper part, and had paid no attention whatever to binding the notes in the bass—I could not believe my eyes and ears!

"We were not so particular," answered Cramer; "we did not consider that of great importance, these are only studies: I have not *your modern* accents and intentions. Clementi played his *Gradus ad Parnassum* just so—it was good enough for us, and no one has ever sung more beautifully on the piano than Field, who was a pupil of Clementi. My pattern was Mozart, no one has ever composed better than he! Now I am forgotten; I'm a poor teacher of the rudiments in a suburb of Paris, where they study the *Bertini Études*, I must even *teach* Bertini myself! You can hear it any time you will—eight pianos going at once!"

I spoke of Hummel, who dedicated to Cramer his *Pianoforte Trio in E major*; I said I thought the theme of the first part fine, but nothing comes of it, except smooth passages.

"Next to Mozart, Hummel is the greatest composer for piano," said Cramer, "no one has surpassed him."

I knew that Cramer could not endure Beethoven, much less Weber: I had removed all my music, so that nothing remained in the room save only J. B.

Chopin

Cramer. I drew forth his four-hand *Sonata in G major* (with the Adagio in C). I had loved to play it with my life-long friend Dinglestaedt, in the happy days of my youth! Cramer wondered that I should know it—he had to look it over again, himself, then played the bass clumsily and roughly, so that all that remained to me was the honor of having sat next the composer! I had never, but once, in my life, experienced so great a disenchantment with so famous an artist: Beethoven's pupil, Ferdinand Ries, whom I heard in Frankfort-on-Main, in the summer of 1827; he was a woodchopper at the piano.

Cramer had a thick-set figure, a full, ruddy countenance, and dark brown eyes; he had the appearance of an Englishman, and English manners. Considering his old age, he was extremely vigorous. "I am a good walker," said he, "I walked all the way from Batignolles to Paris." He stayed until late in the evening, selecting one and another of his oldest compositions, and playing parts of them.

"I don't remember that! I don't know this any more," were his words. I listened with the *greatest reverence*, but I could not be reconciled to his treatment of the piano. It was repulsive. On taking leave, he said: "Receive the blessing of an old man; I owe you an evening such as I had never hoped to enjoy again. I wish sincerely that it may bring you happiness. And so you say, I am *not* quite forgotten?"

"The great virtuoso Henselt plays your *Études* as *repertory*-music, in St. Petersburg; in my native city, Riga, the *Études* lie upon every piano—they will *never perish;* they alone rank with *The Welltempered Clavichord* as a Book of Wisdom; they have never been equalled, and, like Bach's work, can never be laid aside!"

I spoke from my heart. That *Cramer* had visited me, I could, and can still, scarcely believe.

The worthy man died a few years after, in poverty, and forgotten by all! That would never have been the case had he lived in Germany! Cramer is a poet in his *Études*.

In the meantime, Meyerbeer had come to Paris, and was at work on his new opera, the name of which he refused to divulge. It was *l'Africaine*. His arrival was an event in Paris.

Liszt had left his visiting-card with me, with the following words for Chopin written upon it: *Laissez passer, Franz Liszt*. "Present this at Chopin's,"

Chopin

he told me; "you might never succeed in seeing him at all without a *laissez-passer;* that is the custom among authors and artists of the first rank, we cannot afford to lose our time. About two o'clock, go to the Cité d'Orléans, where he lives — where, also, live the Sand, the Viardot, and Dantan"—[the famous caricaturist, who drew a picture of Liszt playing the piano with *four* hands]. "In the evening, these people assemble at the house of a Spanish countess, who is a political refugee. Perhaps Chopin will take you there; but do not ask him to present you to the Sand, he is very mistrustful!"
"He has not your courage, then?"
"No, he has not, *pauvre Frédéric!*"

At last I could go to Chopin!
The Cité d'Orléans was a new structure of large proportions, with a spacious court,—the first undertaking of this description; a collection of apartments, with numbers, and a name (Cité), is always popular with Parisians.
The Cité lay behind the Rue de Provence, in the fashionable quarter of Paris. It looked aristocratic —and that was and is the end and aim of *everything* there!

Great Piano Virtuosos

I gave Liszt's card to the servant in the anteroom; a man-servant is an article of luxury in Paris, a *rarissima avis* in the home of an artist.

The servant said that M. Chopin was not in Paris.

I did not allow myself to be put out, and repeated: "Deliver this card, I will attend to the rest." Chopin soon came out to me, the card in his hand; a young man, of middle height, slim, haggard, with a sad, though very expressive countenance, and elegant Parisian bearing—stood before me. I have seldom, if ever, met with an apparition so entirely engaging. He did not press me to sit down; I stood before him as before a monarch.—"What do you wish? Are you a pupil of Liszt, an artist?" "A friend of Liszt. I wish to have the privilege of studying with you your Mazurkas, which I regard as a Literature; I have already studied several of them with Liszt"—I felt that I had been incautious, but it was too late.

"So?" said Chopin, deliberately, but in his most amiable tone, "why, then, do you need me? Play to me, please, those you have played with Liszt; I have still a few minutes"—he drew an elegant little watch from his pocket; "I was going out—I had forbidden the door to any one, pardon me!"

Chopin

I found myself in the same painful position which I had experienced thirteen years before, with Liszt; another examination? After Liszt, though, I felt I need fear no one, and I had come from St. Petersburg—I went without further ado to the piano, and opened it as though I were quite at home. It was a Pleyel; I had been told that Chopin never used any other instrument. The Pleyel has an easier action than that of any other Parisian manufacture. I struck a chord before seating myself, in order to get the depth of touch,— *le gué*, I called it. This, and the *mot*, seemed to please Chopin; he smiled, leaned wearily against the piano, and his keen eyes looked me directly in the face. I ventured only one glance towards him, and then boldly struck up the *B flat major Mazurka*, the typical one, to which Liszt had noted the variants for me.

I got through well; the *volata* through the two octaves went better than ever before, the instrument ran even easier than my Érard.

Chopin whispered engagingly: "That *trait* is not your own, is it? *He* showed you that! *He* must have his hand in everything; well! he may dare— he plays to *thousands*, I seldom to *one!* Very well,

Great Piano Virtuosos

I will give you lessons—but only twice a week, that is the most I ever give; it will be difficult for me to find three-quarters of an hour." He looked again at the watch. "What are you reading? With what do you occupy yourself in general?" That was a question I was well prepared to answer: "I prefer George Sand, and Jean Jacques, to all other writers," said I, too quickly —he laughed: he was *beautiful* at that moment.

"Liszt told you to say that—I see, you are initiated—so much the better. Only be punctual, everything goes by clockwork with me, my house is like a dove-cote *(pigeonnier)*. I see already that we shall be congenial; a recommendation from Liszt means something; you are the *first* pupil he has recommended to me—we are friends, we shall be comrades."

I always went to him long before my hour, and waited. One lady after another came out, each more beautiful than the others; once it was Mlle. Laure Duperré, the Admiral's daughter; Chopin always accompanied her to the stairs—she was a most lovely woman, tall and straight, like a palm-tree. To her Chopin dedicated two of his most important Nocturnes (*C minor* and *F sharp minor*, Op.

Chopin

48); she was, at that time, his favorite pupil. In the anteroom I often encountered little Filtsch, who, unfortunately, died young. He was then but thirteen years old—a Hungarian genius. *He* understood, *he* played *Chopin!* At a *soirée* at the house of the Duchesse d'Agoult, Liszt said, of Filtsch, in my presence: "When the little one goes on the road, I shall shut up shop." I was jealous of Filtsch, Chopin had eyes only for him. He gave *him* the *Scherzo in B flat minor* (Op. 31); he had forbidden *me* to touch the piece, saying that it was too difficult—he was right, too—but he permitted me to stay when they played it, so I have often heard this charming work in its highest perfection. Filtsch also played the *E minor Concerto;* Chopin accompanied at a second piano, and insisted that the little fellow played it better than himself; I did not believe it! But such was he; he had little physical strength, but no one could approach him in grace and elegance, and if he embellished, it was always the apotheosis of good taste. Only in his earlier years had Chopin given concerts, and won a place in Paris beside Liszt. That is saying much! Now he played only once a year, semi-publicly, to a select circle of his pupils

Great Piano Virtuosos

and adherents, among the flower of the highest society, who took the tickets in advance, and divided them among themselves, as he told me.

"Do you practise on the day of the concert?" I asked him.

"It is a terrible time for me; I do not like publicity, but it is a duty I owe my position. For two weeks I shut myself up, and play Bach. That is my preparation; I do not practise my own compositions."

Chopin was the Phœnix of *intimacy* with the piano. In his Nocturnes and Mazurkas he is unrivalled, downright fabulous. His Mazurkas were Heinrich Heine's songs on the piano! When I told him so, he played abstractedly with the chain of his little watch, which he always kept on the piano during lessons so as not to overstep the three-quarter hour, which passed so quickly!

"Yes, you understand me," said he. "I listen with pleasure, when you play something of mine for the *first* time, for then *you give me ideas;* if you prepare yourself, it is not at all the same—it is then mediocre."

"Liszt said the same thing to me," escaped me.

"Then I do not wonder that you agree with me,"

Chopin

was his piquant and piqued rejoinder. With Liszt, as with Chopin, one had to be extremely cautious, for, in point of sensibility, they were ultra French.

"Of the Mazurkas, Liszt said one must harness a new pianist of the first rank to each one of them."

"Liszt is always right," answered Chopin; "do you think that *I* am satisfied with my own interpretation of the Mazurkas? A few times I *have* been satisfied—in those yearly Concerts, when I have been uplifted by the appreciative atmosphere of the hall. Only *there* must I be heard, once in the year—the rest of the time is for work! There is that *Valse mélancolique*—you will never in your life be able to play it, but because you understand the piece, I will write something in it for you."[8]

Chopin's autographs are rare; he wrote no letters, no notes: "George Sand," he was heard to say, "writes so beautifully, that no one else has any need to write!" *He* went as far as that! that was his way! How prone is Genius to be deluded by woman! How far higher Chopin stood! Chopin will be played when not a line by George Sand will be read. What has this woman, so overrated in France, ever written, of an imperishable nature? But Chopin's Pindaric *Hymns of Victory*, the *Polacca in*

Great Piano Virtuosos

A flat major (to mention this alone), are immortal; they will always belong to the best literature of the piano, but the works of Sand picture the decline of morals, and thus are the reverse of good literature. Chopin was dazzled, prepossessed from the first for the poisonous plant, perhaps because but *one* side of his literary taste had been cultivated, not *all* sides, as was the case with Liszt. It is often so, and the English judge was right, who in every criminal case put the question: "Where is the woman? I don't see the woman!"

I managed with Chopin as one would with a woman, whom one wished, above all things, to please. With Liszt *I* did not *manage* at all, *he* managed *me*, and just exactly as he pleased. Chopin said to me, in one of his confidential moods: "I have but one fault to find with you; that you are a Russian!" Liszt would never have said that; it was one-sided, narrow—but it was a key to his nature. He often made indirect excuses to me; once he said: "Yes, when one understands Beethoven and Weber so; —no Frenchman ever can!"

When I asked him if we might not go to see Duperré, he answered: "Ah—*she* pleased you! I introduce no one! You have nothing to learn from

Chopin

her, you play my things in Weber style, and have learned something from Liszt." Liszt would not have answered so, he would have said: "When do you wish to go?" To be sure Chopin added, by way of excuse: "In a few days I must play the *A flat major Sonata* of Beethoven (Op. 26) to some Russian ladies; I promised to do so. I pray you, come with me, it will be pleasant for me to have you. The ladies will send their carriage for me, and we shall drive *en princes*."

Carriages played an important part in the life of this strange city—even in this circle!

The Russian ladies were the ideally beautiful Baroness Krüdner, and her charming friend, the Countess Schérémetjew; I had been well known to them in St. Petersburg; they never failed to be present at the Sunday matinées at Henselt's, and at all other musicales at the home of Count Wielhorski.

As we drove along the Boulevards, I spoke to Chopin of Henselt. "*He* would be glad to hear you!" "*I* no less glad to hear him!" answered Chopin, heartily. "Will he not come here sometime?" One must always *come*—the Parisians never *went!*

The Baroness' talented daughter was a pupil of Chopin's, also the young Princess Tchernischow,

Great Piano Virtuosos

daughter of the Russian Minister of War. Chopin dedicated his *Prélude in C sharp minor*, Op. 45, to her.

As we rolled over the Boulevards in the luxurious interior of a St. Petersburg calèche, with liveried servants to whom Chopin called my attention, I thought: "It will not soon happen again, that the first and last letters of the musical alphabet will sit side by side in the brilliant sunlight of beautiful Paris!"

Chopin had been sent for, to play the Beethoven *Sonata*—the Variation movement.

How did Chopin play Beethoven's Op. 26? He played it well, but not so well as his own compositions; neatly, but with no contrasts—not like a *romance*, mounting from variation to variation. His *mezzo voce* was a whisper, but he was unapproachable in his *cantilena*, endlessly finished in coherency of construction—ideally beautiful, but *womanish!* Beethoven is a *man*, and never ceases to be a man! Chopin played on a Pleyel—at one time he would never give a lesson on any other instrument; one *had* to have a Pleyel! Every one was charmed; I, too, was charmed—but only by his *tone*, by his *touch*, by his elegance and grace, by his abso-

Chopin

lutely *pure style*. As we drove back together, I was quite sincere when he asked my opinion.

"*I indicate*," he remarked, without any touchiness,— "the listeners must finish the picture."

When we returned to the house, he went into a small cabinet which adjoined the drawing-room, to change his clothes. I seated myself at the Pleyel. I felt I owed Liszt something, and played the Beethoven theme so as to express an autumn landscape, with a dash of summer sunlight! with the three well-graduated, very intensive *crescendos* in the five consecutive A flats (sixteenth-note groups). Everything that was in it, came forth, even to a sudden halt before the *gruppetto* in thirty-second notes! Chopin came at once from the cabinet, and sat down near me, still in his shirt-sleeves. I played well, and glowed like a coal; it was a sort of challenge, but not intentionally so; I but spoke with myself. At the Thema, I stopped, and looked him quietly in the eyes. He laid his hand on my shoulder, and said: "I will tell Liszt. It never occurred to me to play it like that, but it is *fine*. But must one *always* speak with so much passion?"—"It is no drawing-room piece, it is the life of a human being," I replied; "Rochlitz has written a novel about it; and that it must be played with passion, is signified in the coda of the last variation, where the B flats are only an accompaniment to the Aspiration, are no longer dotted, and are played in the middle. But what do *you* not do with the groups of triplets in the last variation? If I could only learn *that* of you! But that would be impossible, that is a part of your nature, and belongs to your peculiar management of the instrument!"

We talked much of Beethoven, for the first time. He never cared very much for Beethoven; he only knew his great compositions, nothing at all of his last works. That was in the air of Paris! The Symphonies were known there; the Quartets but little—the later ones, not at all. The *Morin Quartet Society* was formed later; Paris was always decades behind Germany.

I told Chopin, among other things: In the *F minor Quartet* Beethoven had divined Mendelssohn, Schumann, and *him* [Chopin]; the Scherzo prepared one for *his Mazurka Fantasias;* this did not mean, in the least, that *he* had borrowed from Beethoven; Beethoven embraced *all* within himself—a universal genius like that, anticipates future epochs in this way.[9]

Chopin

"Bring me that Quartet," said Chopin, "I do not know it." I brought it. He thanked me repeatedly. I also brought Weber. He did not appreciate him; he spoke of "Opera," of "unklaviermässig" [bad piano-style]!—In general, Chopin was far from comprehending the German spirit in music, though I often heard him say: "There *is* but *one School*, the *German*." The build of his compositions is German, not French; he bears Bach in mind. Of many examples, let us consider the *C sharp minor Mazurka*, Op. 50, and the *C sharp minor Mazurka*, Op. 4: they begin as though written for the organ, and end in an exclusive salon; they are in imitative style. They do him much credit. They are more fully worked out than usual — they are sonnets, as were none of the others!—Chopin was much pleased when I told him that, in the construction of *Mazurka* Op. 50, the passage from E major to F major was the same as that in the *Agatha Aria* of *Robin des bois* (compare, in the *C major Sonata* of Weber, the Trio of the *Menuetto* in *E major*, eight measures before the close).

"I do not know the *Aria*, though I have heard it—show it to me." When I brought him the *Aria* and *Sonata* he said: "I did not know that anything like this had ever been written!" "And think how long ago Weber wrote them," I answered, "the Sonata in 1813, the *Freischütz* in 1820!"

. . . .

I tormented Chopin most, with the famous *Nocturne* in E flat major, Op. 9, dedicated to the lovely Camille Pleyel. He, like Liszt, was very sensible to the charms of women.

>*Deux coqs vivaient en paix, une poule survint :*
>*Et voilà la guerre allumée.*
>*Amour! tu perdis Troie!*

The *Nocturne* is simply a perfected Field, grafted on a more interesting bass; in 1842 it was in the full bloom of fashion; now it is superseded by the later, the higher forms in Chopin—more especially by the Duperré *Nocturnes*, Op. 48 (C minor and F sharp minor).

When Chopin was pleased with a scholar, he, with a small, well-sharpened pencil, made a cross under the composition. I had received one, in the *Nocturne (premier chevron)*; next time I came, I got another. I came still another time. "Do please let me alone," said Chopin, "I do not like the piece at

Chopin

all [because he had already soared beyond it]; there, you have another cross, *more* than three I *never* give. *You* cannot do it any better!"

"You play it so beautifully," I ventured, "can no one else?" "Liszt can," said Chopin, drily, and played it to me no more. He had noted in it some very important little changes for me; his notes were clean, small, and sharp, like English diamond type.

In the Cité d'Orléans, where Chopin lived, lived also Dantan, George Sand, and Pauline Viardot. They assembled in the evening, in the same house, in the apartment of an old Spanish countess, a political *émigrée*. All of which Liszt had told me. Chopin took me with him once. On the stairs he said: "You must play something, but nothing of mine—play your Weber piece" (the *Invitation*).

George Sand said not a word when Chopin introduced me. That was uncivil. For that reason, I immediately sat down close to her. Chopin hovered round like a frightened bird in a cage, he saw that something was coming. Was there ever a time when he was without apprehension in her presence? At the first pause in the conversation, which was conducted by Sand's friend, Madame Viardot (I was to become well acquainted with this great singer, later, in St. Petersburg), Chopin took me by the arm, and led me to the piano. Reader! If you play the piano, you can picture to yourself how sorely I stood in need of courage! It was a *Pleyel upright*, which, in Paris, passed for a pianoforte! I played "The Invitation" fragmentarily; Chopin shook me by the hand; George Sand did not say a word. I sat down by her, again, and followed my purpose openly. Chopin regarded us apprehensively, across the table, on which the inevitable *carcel* was burning.

"Will you not come to St. Petersburg sometime?" said I, in my politest manner, to George Sand, "where you are read so much, and so highly respected." "I will never lower myself, by visiting a country where slavery exists," she answered shortly. *(Je ne m'abaisserai jamais jusqu'à un pays d'esclaves!)*

This was indecent, after she had been discourteous.

"After all, you may be right, *not* to come," I replied, in the same tone: "you might find the door closed against you! I just thought of Kaiser Nikolaus." George Sand looked at me, astounded; I looked steadily back, into her beautiful, big, brown cow-eyes. Chopin did not seem displeased. I understood every motion of his head.

Chopin

Instead of answering, George Sand rose, and strode like a man across the room to the glowing fire.

I followed at her heels, and sat down, ready primed, next her—for the third time.

She had to say something, at last.

She drew an enormously thick Trabucco cigar from her apron-pocket, and called back, into the drawing-room: "*Frédéric, un fidibus!*"

I felt insulted in him—my great lord and master; I understood Liszt's remark: *Pauvre Frédéric!* in all its bearings.

Chopin obediently brought a *fidibus*.

After the first abominable whiff of smoke, George Sand favored me with a question: "I suppose I could not even smoke a cigar in a drawing-room in St. Petersburg?"

"In *no* drawing-room, Madame, have I ever seen a cigar smoked," I answered, not without emphasis, with a bow!

She looked at me sharply, the thrust had struck home! I looked quietly around at the fine pictures in the salon, each one of which was lighted up by a separate lamp. Chopin had probably not overheard us, he had returned to the table, where our hostess sat.

Great Piano Virtuosos

Pauvre Frédéric!—how sorry I was for him—the great artist!

The next day, M. Armand, the *portier* of my hotel, said to me: "A gentleman and lady have been here—I told them you were not at home,—you did not say you wished to receive visitors. The gentleman had no card, but left his name." I read: *Chopin et Madame George Sand*. I quarrelled every day for two months, with M. Armand.

Such are the Parisians; one must know beforehand, if one is to have visitors—and it nearly always happens, that visitors come at such inconvenient times, that one has to be denied to them!

That truly would have been an interesting visit! Chopin might even have played with me! I should have *made* him.

Chopin said to me, during my lesson: "George Sand [Mme. Dudevant was always so called] went with me to see you—what a pity you were not at home! I regretted it very much. She felt that she had been rude to you! You would have seen how amiable she can be; you pleased her very much!"

The Spanish countess probably had a hand in that visit; she was a woman of distinction, and she may have reproved George Sand for her rudeness to me

Chopin

—I thought. I drove to call upon George Sand; she was not in. I asked: "What is Madame properly called—Dudevant?" "Ah! Monsieur, she has many names," was the concièrge's answer.

From that time on, Chopin was particularly complaisant to me. I had pleased George Sand! That was a diploma. George Sand had considered me worthy the honor of a visit! That was promotion! Liszt or Chopin—humanity is the same everywhere.

"You are approved," Liszt had said to me a month earlier, referring to a Parisian lady of the highest rank, whom he had always wished to please, and had always succeeded in pleasing! But I had only told the lady of Liszt's triumph in St. Petersburg, a thing he could not very well do himself.

Herein we all resemble one another—*hic jacet homo!* —The following incident was entirely characteristic of Liszt. After I had told the above-mentioned lady the story of Liszt's triumph, she had invited me— simply out of courtesy—to play Weber to her. Liszt found me still at the piano, and said: "You replace me *also* at the piano"—(*Vous me faites donc des queues au piano?*) half in jest, half in earnest, as always with him—and as always with everything in Paris!

Great Piano Virtuosos

I have already touched on the altogether charming —but not *great*—style of Chopin's playing; quite inimitable, for example, in his so-called Waltzes, which waltzes are enchanted rondos, of a kind unknown before. Once Meyerbeer came in while I was taking my lesson with Chopin. I had never seen him before. Meyerbeer was not announced; he was a king. I was just playing the *Mazurka in C*, Op. 33 —on only one page, which contains so many hundreds; I named it the "Epitaph of the Idea"—so full of grief and sorrow is this composition—the weary flight of an eagle!

Meyerbeer had seated himself; Chopin let me play on.

"That is two-four time," said Meyerbeer.

For reply, Chopin made me repeat, and kept time by tapping loudly upon the instrument with his pencil; his eyes glowed.

"Two-four," Meyerbeer repeated quietly.

I never but once saw Chopin angry; it was at this time! A delicate flush colored his pale cheeks, and he looked very handsome.

"It is three-four," he said *loudly*, he, who always spoke so softly!

"Give it me, for a ballet for my opera *(l'Africaine*, then kept a secret), I will show you, *then!*"

Chopin

"It is *three*-four," almost screamed Chopin, and played it himself. He played it several times, counted aloud, and stamped the time with his foot—he was beside himself! It was of no use, Meyerbeer insisted it was two-four, and they parted in ill humor. It was anything but agreeable to me to have witnessed this little scene. Chopin disappeared into his cabinet without saying a word—the whole thing had lasted but a couple of minutes. I introduced myself to Meyerbeer, as the friend of his friend, Count Wielhorski in St. Petersburg. "May I take you home?" he kindly asked, as he stood on the platform in the court, where his coupé awaited him. We were hardly seated, when he began: "I had not seen Chopin in a long time, I love him dearly! I know no pianist like him, no composer for piano like him! The piano is intended for delicate shading, for the *cantilena*, it is an instrument for close intimacy. I also was a pianist, once, and there was a time when I aspired to be a virtuoso; come and see me, when you come to Berlin—we are now comrades; when people meet under the roof of such a great man, it is for life." Meyerbeer spoke German, and so heartily! He pleased me far more than the Parisians; but Chopin was right. Though the third beat in the composition referred to is slurred over, it no less exists, but I took good care not to press this point against the composer of *Les Huguenots*.

Et adhuc sub judice lis est!

When I met Meyerbeer in Berlin, twenty years later, the first thing he said was: "Do you still remember? It was during your lesson that I interrupted."

"You hurt his feelings! What must Chopin have felt, when *you* denied the triple rhythm to a composition which is substantially founded on that rhythm —and then consider his irritability!"

"I did not intend to be unkind," said the great man, good-naturedly, "I thought he wished it so!"

That which particularly characterized Chopin's playing was his *rubato*, whereby the rhythm and time through the whole remained accurate. "The left hand," I often heard him say, "is the conductor, it must not waver, or lose ground; do with the right hand what you will and can." He taught: "Supposing that a piece lasts a given number of minutes; it may take just so long to perform the whole, but in the details deviations may occur!"

But I heard Chopin's *rubato* better defined, by Liszt, at Weimar in 1871—as I heard from his distin-

Chopin

guished pupil, the capital Russian pianist Neilissow. "Do you see those trees?" Liszt said to Neilissow; "The wind plays in the leaves, Life unfolds and develops beneath them; but the *tree remains the same*—that is the Chopin *rubato!*"

In the fluctuation of the tempo, in this "Hangen und Bangen"—in the *rubato* of his conception, Chopin was ravishing; every note stood on the highest degree of taste, in the noblest sense of that term. When he embellished—which he rarely did—it was always a species of miracle of good taste. In his entire make-up, Chopin was not fitted to interpret Beethoven or Weber, who paint along great lines with great brushes. Chopin was a painter of pastels, but an *unrivalled* one. Contrasted with Liszt he might stand on an honorable equality with him—as his wife. The grand *B flat major* of Beethoven, Op. 106, and Chopin, are mutually exclusive.

About this time there lived in Paris a pianist by the name of Gutmann; a rough fellow at the piano, but with robust health, and a herculean frame. Through these physical endowments, he impressed Chopin—the Sand also extended to him her protection. Chopin praised Gutmann as the pianist whose interpretation of his compositions was most grateful to him!

Great Piano Virtuosos

That *was* strong! He said "he had taught himself." That was stronger, *he*, a giant! The *Scherzo in C sharp minor*, Op. 39, is dedicated to Gutmann, and Chopin certainly had his prize-fighter fist in mind, when he composed it, for no left hand can take the chord in the bass (sixth measure, *d* sharp, *f* sharp, *g*, *d* sharp, *f* sharp), least of all Chopin's hand, which arpeggio'd over the easy-running, narrow-keyed Pleyel. Only Gutmann could "knock a hole in a table" with *that* chord! I heard him at Chopin's; he played like a porter; so does Genius allow itself to be deluded, when its own weaknesses sit in judgment! To the little Filtsch, and me, Gutmann was a horror; we derided him; he learned absolutely nothing of Chopin, though Chopin took so much trouble to try and carve a toothpick out of this log! That was sufficient to blindfold him. Nothing more was ever heard of this Gutmann—he was a discovery of Chopin's.

Chopin died of a broken heart, not of consumption; he died at the same age as Mozart and Raphael. Liszt wrote a delightful book—*Frédéric Chopin, by Franz Liszt*, it is called; a speaking title. It was published in 1845 by Escudier, in Paris, and the entire edition was sold out. I was unable to procure

Chopin

a copy, either in Berlin, Leipzig, or St. Petersburg, whither a great number of them had been shipped —I had to read it by snatches, in the library of Count Wielhorski. It has been repeatedly asked for in Paris, but always in vain.

George Sand speaks of Chopin in her book, "*Un hiver au midi de l'Europe;*" it is a description of her sojourn in Minorca, with Chopin, whom the Parisian doctors had sent to the Balearics, he being already dangerously ill with consumption. She does not mention his name, she speaks of him as *l'Artiste*. That is singularly secret! It is not depreciating, but, for so great an artist, neither is it sufficiently appreciative; it is simply, *foolishly Parisian!* How could a French nature understand Chopin? A Sand could never take a loftier flight in music than: "*Jouez-moi quelque chose, Frédéric! un fidibus, Frédéric!*" etc. *L'Artiste* was caught in a web, to which the spider was not lacking!

The compositions of Chopin opened a new era for the pianoforte. They run the risk, through lack of knowledge of the master's style of playing, of his intentions, of his views concerning the pianoforte, of remaining misunderstood; because there is infinitely more in the playing of them than appears on the

Great Piano Virtuosos

printed page. In expressing the inner soul of the instrument, and in their treatment of the same, they must be ranked above Weber. They went a step further. They maintain a *first place* in piano-literature. They occupy the plane of ideas of a Novalis, a Heine. They cannot be "arranged" for any other instrument; they are the Soul of the Piano. They are less in touch with *general* musical ideas than with *piano*-ideas. They are often *great* works in *small* frames — they are elegiac — lyric — on the standpoint of their creator's nationality; yet they are ideal, they are imperishable in the history of musical thought.

It is not my purpose to discuss the compositions of Chopin; it would be impossible to do so, within the small compass of these pages. A pamphlet is not a book. Only a book would suffice to give a complete picture of such great personalities as those of Liszt and Chopin, those *Dioscuri* of the modern pianoforte. Such a picture would necessarily include a complete historical view of art and literature as it was in the thirties and forties. The writers of that day were Balzac and Hugo, Dumas and Sue, Guizot and Villemain; the painters, Ary Scheffer and Delacroix; the composers, Cherubini, Rossini, Halévy

Chopin

and Berlioz. They all belong to that historic view of civilization.

Only in this focus of light could the forms of Liszt and Chopin appear in life-size.

In comparison to the later condition of French affairs—the total Napoleonic eclipse—the days of the Louis Philippe régime were a great epoch. "*Notre voix avait un son éclatant qu'elle a perdu,*" Jules Janin wrote me, at St. Petersburg in 1853.

Musical literature is a concrete form of the activity of universal mental culture, and hence a mirror of the life, amid whose conditions it had its origin.

The works of Chopin are no exception; even Chopin is a.son of his time, and only through the history of that time will he be understood. One can make an absolute estimate of Bach, Haydn, Mozart, and Beethoven, but *not* of Weber, even.

Let us glance at the compositions of Chopin. We must exclaim: *so much* in *so little!* in barely sixty-four authentic opus-numbers, of which the "first steps" are a negligeable quantity.—And yet so much in the domain of Mind!

What *could* one *not* say about the finished technique of Chopin? in which regard he even ranks above

Great Piano Virtuosos

Weber! What cannot one say about his style of writing, his harmony, his modulation, his treatment of the piano in general, and especially of the left hand?[10]

Chopin's tone-color is like that of Raphael! He is the Raphael of the piano—though one must not seek his Madonnas in the churches—but in Life!

Carl Tausig

Dem Mann muss Musik-
feuer aus'm Kopf schlagen —
Rührung passt für Weiber
　　　　　　　BEETHOVEN

Carl Tausig

SELDOM has a death excited such universal sympathy as did that of Carl Tausig, cut off, like Chopin, at the very height of his artistic career, in the strongest period of his musical development!

People who formed no part in the musical world, who had never heard Tausig, but had only heard of him, felt the loss which all experienced, who honored in Tausig not alone the artist, but the man. In St. Petersburg, where Tausig had appeared but once, every one spoke of the sad death in Leipsic, as though it were one of their own near and dear ones who had entered the spiritual life. How much more must this have been the case in Germany!

There was but one opinion of Tausig, even among the envious!—unfortunately there are such among us musicians, whether we scratch paper with pens, or play piano, or scrape, or blow; only the thumper (Timpani!) is harmless—and not even he, in Vienna, where he is a piano-virtuoso to boot!

There are men who, upon their first appearance among us, make a lasting impression. To these few belonged Tausig.

Great Piano Virtuosos

In the late autumn of 1868 I was on my way towards Europe's stronghold of Reason, Berlin—with the purpose of hearing Tausig. I was leaving behind me that charming butterfly-casket, Dresden, where one finds everything—as in a surgeon's case—excepting caliber.

I had had in Dresden such a variety of thoughts concerning the greatness of the composer of *Der Freischütz* in the theatre, and at the piano, that I was too preoccupied in arranging them to take precautionary measures against the harvest-wind blowing across the stubble, and felt ill by the time we reached the lines of lamps which told me that we were nearing Berlin; in contrast to the dimness of the Saxon nights, these lights appeared like an illumination in honor of some royal event! Berlin's caliber already began to assert itself.

My artistic friend, the General-Intendant, Herr von Hülsen, had promised to give, that evening—at my request—*Der Freischütz*, from which I had not been separated for the past forty years. He wished to notice my little polemic concerning the performance of this manifestation of German Mind, so he had given orders that my observations should be considered; he particularly asked: "We surely have not four

Carl Tausig

trombones in *Der Freischütz?*" At Dresden, the introduction of the *tuba* in Weber's music struck me like a cuckoo's egg—quite anti-Weber in effect. No tuba, *mirum spargens sonum*, but with the suggestion, not the real introduction of the wind-instruments, as in Mozart's *Requiem*.[11]

Herr von Hülsen had kindly offered me his box, and the fatality which attends a traveller brought me there long before the time. I raised the green screen and looked down into the orchestra, where but two people appeared in the semi-darkness, a viola and a clarinet. Said the viola to the clarinet: "Look sharp now! draw back well on the dominant in the Overture, as we have been told; *he* is already here"—pointing out my hiding-place behind the screen. *That* was *caliber:* the consideration of a possible truth which *he* had not grasped!

I was soon quite ill, and obliged to keep my room. I wrote Tausig, whom I did not personally know, to say how much I regretted my inability to call upon him. In but a few hours a young man, somewhat under middle height and delightfully unaffected—stood before me. "I am Tausig; as you were unable to come to me, I came to you—I will come twice every day, if I can. You are of Liszt's household, so

Great Piano Virtuosos

am I—we are comrades, and I am at your command while you are in Berlin." Chopin did not receive me in this manner; this was Berlin, not Paris! That was German cordiality, no conventional iciness about that—and yet Tausig occupied the same position in Berlin, as did Chopin in Paris.[12]

"Shall I send you a piano?" he asked. "I have some very good ones."

I was soon able to visit him in the Taubenstrasse, where he lived. The first time I went he was not at home. I told the maid I would await her master, and made my way directly to the bookcase in the first room. On the handsome bindings in the first row I read the names of the great German philosophers. I was less astounded, than pleasantly surprised. I had to wait a long while, so I examined one book after another until I came to Arthur Schopenhauer, when Tausig laid his hand on my shoulder saying: "Good books, are they not? They are my favorites—and they are not for show, I read them often! Down here are my 'naturals'—(he spoke jestingly of the natural histories)—but your book is also here; do you not believe me?—here it is."

"Have you read it?—truly?"

He hesitated a moment, then looked me frankly in

Carl Tausig

the eyes and said: "I have read the French one; it made a fearful row at Liszt's."

"That is the poorest one," I replied; "read the German one—but only the last volume is for you—the contemplation of the last works—for instance the *A major Sonata*, Op. 101; Holz and others in Vienna supplied me with some hitherto unknown particulars concerning it."

"The *A major* is in that? It is my favorite. That shall be 'taken care of.' I will read it to-day." He took down the book, and laid it on the table in the drawing-room.

We went into the next room, where the first piano presented itself. On this the *Quasi-Fantasia in C sharp* lay open. "A pupil has forgotten this," said Tausig.

"Did you know that that should be played only in a room draped in black?"

"No, I did not know that, at all!"

"Holz wrote me about it, he knows it; Beethoven confided to him that he improvised the Adagio while sitting beside the corpse of a friend in a room hung with black."

"That is just lovely!" laughed Tausig, in his humorous manner; "if a pupil ever again torments me with

Great Piano Virtuosos

it, I shall ask: 'Is your room hung with black, nothing but black? Not otherwise.'"[3]

In this, my first visit, the piano played no part, I avoided it purposely. Tausig said: "Well, we have always known each other, and you shall come every day. If you should hear a piano-racket when you come in, that's the pupils! Escape into my study—there stands my best piano, there you will find scores, the newspapers and, *I* think, the best cigars in Berlin. If you still hear the din, you must play against it; that is what I do, for other people give lessons at my house—I am *collective*, you see; but I can't stand it long; only one more lustrum, and I'm off to the University to amuse myself with the study of philosophy and natural history, and to live, as far as possible—without a piano. Will you come with me? What do you think of Heidelberg? Berlin is wearing, have you not yet noticed that? But I am *very* fond of Berlin—still—only five more years of this 'collective' business, and I shall say: '*Johanna geht, und nimmer kehrt sie wieder!*'" That was characteristic of Tausig—how far removed from the brazen bonds of fashion in Paris!

At my second visit, Tausig played me the *A major Sonata*, Op. 101—as I had never before heard it;

the first movement became an idyl; his handling of the finale with the fugue, was a revelation. "The second theme, in the finale just before the fugue, you divide between two wind-instruments; I heard —so to speak—the oboe," I observed.

"How glad I am! that, in fact, is my intention— but I never told any one."

"The *nuance* in touch tells it," I replied.

He seemed pleased.

"The first movement may be given *quasi chitarra*," I remarked.

"Two guitars, or four, if you like!" He played the movement so that I could hear the guitars, and said: "But our *legato* is better, let us keep to the grand style—Beethoven was no painter of genre-pictures —I will now play you Chopin's *A flat major Polonaise*—it is a little specialty of mine!"

I never heard this triumphal, stupendously difficult piece in such perfection, played with such easy mastery over, or rather, with such complete obliviousness to, the mechanical difficulties. The Trio, in descending octaves for the left hand, aroused an astonishment to which I gave unstinted expression:

"That is beyond everything!" I cried, "how can you play those octaves so evenly, so sonorously—in that furious tempo? Murmuring pianissimo, thunderous fortissimo?"

"I told you that it is a specialty! Look, my hand is small, and I hold it still closer together; my left hand is so formed that it runs by itself over the four degrees, *e*, *d* sharp, *c* sharp, *b*—it's a kind of *lusus naturæ*" (smiling); "I can do it as long as you like —it does not tire me; that was written for me. Strike these four octaves with *both* hands; you can't play them so loud." I tried it. "See! see! very good, but not as loud as mine, and after a couple of measures you are tired—and so are the octaves! I do not think any one else can play this passage just as I do—but how few understand it! It is the tramp of the horses in the Polish Light Cavalry!"

To me, the supreme artistic moment was the exposition of the principal motive, at every entrance. It was the Poles, drunk with victory, sweeping away their beautiful partners in the dance!

"I have heard *three* scales played, in my lifetime; Tausig in this *Polonaise*, Liszt in Beethoven's *Scherzo*, Op. 106, and Henselt in Chopin's *A minor Étude*; these are the Amazon streams of the piano, they overspread its entire extent, and are inimitable!"

Carl Tausig

Tausig answered: "No mortal can vie with Liszt; he dwells upon a solitary height!"

"Do you also play Weber?" I asked.

"I do not like to. I do not care to expose my inmost self to the public, and that is what Weber demands, does he not? I play for the sake of Art, and I believe that when I have satisfied *her*, I have also satisfied mankind! The *Concertstück*, however, I have often played, but it is not within my province, like Beethoven's *E flat major Concerto*—that is my specialty; I shall play that at my *début* in St. Petersburg. The Philharmonics have written for me —who are they? I shall play at their concert, and will give my own self."

"The Philharmonics, as you call them, are a society, an old society, of St. Petersburg musicians who give two concerts yearly, in the Hall of the Nobles, for the benefit of their widows and orphans."

"I will come, that is 'taken care of;' I must see St. Petersburg. Do you play Beethoven much?"

"Not oftener than I go to church (Tausig smiled slyly), which one ordinarily does in moderation. One reads Beethoven, has read him often, will read him again and again. The *actual* Beethoven lives in the orchestra."

Great Piano Virtuosos

"About Weber," said Tausig, "I have designs on the *Invitation;* I wish to work on it, and should like to talk with you about it. At my house we should be often disturbed. I frequently can find a free hour in the midst of my business, if you would wait for me? there are suitable meeting-places."

I proposed the *Maison Dorée* on *Unter den Linden*. There we met and talked undisturbed. I admired the modesty of the great artist; his eagerness to hear about Chopin, whose acquaintance he had never had the opportunity to make, and yet whose works he interpreted as no other could!

I told Tausig of Chopin's peculiar treatment of that innocent *Nocturne in E flat*, Op. 9, No. 2.

"That is interesting," said Tausig, "I will play through the bass with *both* hands, myself; that is the place for the guitar—that shall be 'taken care of.'"

But he was most interested in the fact of Chopin being so critical and hard to please in the first four measures of the great *C minor Nocturne* (Op. 48, No. 1, Lento)—apparently so simple. In the second measure occurs the sixteenth-note figure *d*, *e* flat, *f*, *g*. The point was, to glide from this *g* to *c*, in the third measure. Chopin was never satisfied with this.

Carl Tausig

He said to me: "It is possible for you to do this, so you *must* do it." At last I was able to satisfy him, but it took a long while—sometimes the g was too short, and changed to the c too quickly—sometimes it was just the other way. "There is a meaning in it," Chopin said. It was just as difficult to please with the lifting of the c before the eighth-note rest in the sixteenth-note group e flat, c, in the fourth measure; the c was always too short or too long! I found a way out by drawing my finger along the key until I came to the end, and then drawing it off at the sharp corner; at last he was satisfied! But it was nothing when compared to the manner in which Chopin played both these passages!

"I quite understand him," remarked Tausig, "I shall 'take care of' that."

"Chopin intended the passage from g to c as a question; c gave the answer."

"So I understood it," said Tausig.

Just as rarely was Chopin satisfied with the first measure in the *C minor Nocturne;* the quarter-notes g, a flat, should be prominent, being thematic, but they were always too *forte* or too *piano*. Chopin always used a Pleyel, an instrument with light

Great Piano Virtuosos

action, on which one can do such shading much more easily than on one of mellower, fuller tone.

During the next few days, Tausig played me both Nocturnes in the most finished manner, in fact, just as Chopin played them. He was pleased himself, and said: "I ought to have known Him!" Never was a composer so lovingly cherished by a virtuoso, as was Chopin by Tausig.

One day Tausig appeared at my rooms early in the morning: "The Baroness Schweinitz invites you to a *soirée* at her house; she is my best pupil—indeed, I can scarcely call her a pupil, she is an artist, and a charming woman. You will meet interesting people there. The Baroness sends her excuses that the Baron has not called on you."

"I do not stand upon ceremony, and consider myself honored by the invitation," was my reply.

"Then I will be here this evening at eight sharp, and we will drive to the Commandant's house."

As we went through the vestibule into the large, half-lit stuccoed hall, I said: "We have such halls in St. Petersburg, but not many."

"I have often played here," said Tausig; "we give charity concerts here, in which the Baroness takes the lead."

Carl Tausig

Tausig walked to a side-door of mahogany, richly gilded, and opened it. A suite of three salons, bright as day, lay before us; in the first, we were most winningly received by the Baroness. The gathering consisted of several distinguished artists belonging to the musical circle of Tausig and the Baroness; the Austrian Ambassador, Count Wimpffen, and his wife; the Russian military plenipotentiary, Count Kutusow; and the master of the house, Court Minister von Schweinitz. Tausig had not said too much; in a composition of Schumann's, and a difficult, brilliant piece of Tausig's, the Baroness proved herself a finished artist. Tausig's demeanor particularly pleased me: he quite effaced himself—it was as though he were not there at all, and yet he was everywhere, and the life of the animated conversation. This *soirée* lives among my musico-social memories as one equally distinguished for intellectuality and good taste. Since the death of the great artist who amiably opened these doors to me, the memory of it has become a sacred one. In the higher circles of St. Petersburg, Berlin has a reputation for stiffness of etiquette. Here was one of the best houses in Berlin opened to me, a stranger, whose only recommendation was, being known to Tausig.

Great Piano Virtuosos

As we drove home, Tausig said: "You have given me uncommon pleasure! You sat at the piano just as *He* does."—

"You cannot believe that it ever occurred to me to imitate Liszt?" I was somewhat disconcerted—what could Tausig mean?

"You do not understand me; I am in earnest; there is no imitation about it, only an affinity in the spirit of the matter, understood by myself alone;—not at all the way you sat there—something to which you gave no thought in your intercourse with the piano; it was *He*, as he lives and moves, I tell you, and I could think only of *Him* the whole evening!"

Seldom is a master so lovingly reverenced by a pupil, as Liszt by Tausig! He had such a true, loyal, loving heart! Such an amiable nature should never have been wounded in its inner life, in the most sensitive spot. In Tausig's character humanism was prominent, like the artistic height on which he stood. Dark clouds seemed to have gathered early over his life; the artist took refuge from them in his Art, his virtuosity was a veil behind which the artist sought to conceal the man—in other words, to mould his art objectively. In his daily life he regarded as a simple human duty, what others call

Carl Tausig

worshipping God. Not with any desire to shine, but with an earnest purpose, did Tausig take up the study of philosophy; he was far from caring for ostentation, he never courted applause—it was quite indifferent to him: a fact I had good opportunity to observe at his triumphs in St. Petersburg. Melancholy, a certain profundity of meditation, which caused him to appear absent-minded, while his thoughts were but too vividly actual,—dominated him; he tried to conceal the underlying vein of sadness, but it was clearly evident, and the dash of humor in his conversation was also the flight of his spirit before the gloomy spectre, the *atra cura* of Horace! I found a key to his artistic nature in the manner in which he approached the *Barcarole* of Chopin. "Do you know the Barcarole?" he asked me.

"No!"

"I will play it to you on Sunday; but come early, before the hour my friends, Messrs. Davidsohn and C. F. Weitzmann, and some on the staff of *Kladderadatsch*,[14] usually drop in. This is between ourselves; it is an interpretation which must not be attempted before more than two people; I will disclose *myself* to you—I love the piece, but I seldom play it."

Great Piano Virtuosos

That same day I read the Barcarole through carefully, at a music-store. The piece did not please me at all; a long composition in nocturne-style, bombastic in tonality (Fsharp major) and modulation; a tower of figuration reared on an insecure foundation! And the greatest mechanical difficulties into the bargain—well, the latter were Tausig's affair!

How sadly was I at fault!

Tausig explained the piece, which, as an exception, he did not play by heart:—"This tells of two persons, of a love-scene in a secret gondola; we might call this *mise en scène* symbolic of lover's meetings in general. That is expressed in the thirds and sixths; the dual character of two notes (persons) runs through the whole—it is all two-voiced, or two-souled. In this modulation into C sharp major (marked *dolce sfogato*) one recognizes a kiss and an embrace—that is plain enough! When, after three measures of introduction, this bass solo—an easy rocking theme—enters in the fourth, and this theme is, nevertheless, employed only as an accompaniment throughout the entire composition; on this lies the *cantilena* in two voices, and we have a sweet and long dialogue. From the chain of double trills on,

Carl Tausig

the story becomes difficult to tell—*that* is my affair, I'll 'take care of' that. Turn the leaves well and listen attentively."

Seldom in my life have I heard so sweet, such a wonderfully beautiful story told at the piano. Every note spoke, the artist gave way to the man in Tausig; and how interesting were both!

How difficult, how impossible, except to subjective interpretation, it is to carry through nine pages of enervating music, in the same long-breathed rhythm (twelve-eighths) so much interest, so much emotion, so much action, that I regretted that the long piece was not longer!

Tausig was here the living impersonation of Chopin, he played like him, he felt as he did, he *was* Chopin at the piano!

I told him so frankly, and he felt the sincerity of conviction in my words. But he was always careful, even suspicious, on such occasions, perhaps because he was never of a merry disposition, never able entirely to dissipate his clouds!

Tausig gave concerts in Berlin which were entirely devoted to Chopin's compositions, the first instance of such a thing, I think—excepting the yearly *concerts intimes* given in Paris by the master himself.

Great Piano Virtuosos

How thankless undertakings of this sort usually are! How grateful we should be to Tausig for taking such an initiative with regard to Chopin, whose pianistic importance is by far too lightly estimated. Tausig also impressed me deeply in his interpretation of Chopin's *Ballade* in F minor. It has three requirements: "The comprehension of the programme as a whole—for Chopin writes according to programme, to the situations in life best known to, and understood by, himself; the exposition of the motives in detail, and in an adequate manner; the conquest of the stupendous difficulties in complicated figures, winding harmonies and formidable passages."

Tausig fulfilled these requirements, presenting an embodiment of the signification and the feeling of the work. The Ballade (*andante con moto*, six-eighths) begins in the minor key of the dominant; the seventh measure comes to a stand before a *fermata* on C major. The easy handling of these seven measures Tausig interpreted thus: "The piece has not yet begun;" in his firmer, nobly expressive exposition of the principal theme, free from sentimentality (to which one might easily yield), the "grand style" found due scope.

Carl Tausig

An essential requirement in an instrumental virtuoso is that he should understand how to breathe, and how to allow his hearers to take breath—giving them opportunity to arrive at a better understanding. By this I mean a well-chosen incision, the *cæsura*, and a *lingering* ("letting in air," Tausig cleverly called it) which in no way impairs rhythm and time, but rather brings them into stronger relief: a *lingering* which our signs of notation cannot adequately express,[15] because it is made up of atomic time-values. Rub the bloom from a peach or from a butterfly; that which remains will belong to the kitchen, to natural history!—It is not otherwise with Chopin; the bloom consisted in Tausig's treatment of the Ballade.

He came to the first passage,—as one would ordinarily say; the motive from among blossoms and leaves, as one must say for Chopin—a figurated recurrence of the principal theme is in the inner parts—its polyphonic variant. A little thread connects this with the chorale-like introduction of the second theme. The theme is strongly and abruptly modulated, perhaps a little too much so. Tausig tied the little thread to a *doppio movimento* in two-four time, but thereby resulted sextolets, which threw the chorale into yet bolder relief. Then followed a passage *a tempo*, in which the principal theme played hide-and-go-seek.

How clear it all became, as Tausig played it! Of technical difficulties he knew literally nothing; the intricate and evasive parts were as easy as the easiest—I might say, easier!

I admired the short trills in the left hand, which were trilled out quite independently, as if by a second player; the gliding ease of the cadence marked *dolcissimo*. It swung itself into the higher register, where it came to a stop before A major, just as the introduction stopped before C major. Then, after the theme has once more presented itself in a modified form (variation), it comes under the pestle of an extremely figurate coda, which demands the study of an artist, the strength of a robust man—the most vigorous pianistic health, in a word!

Tausig overcame this threatening group of terrific difficulties, whose appearance in the piece is well explained by the programme, without the slightest effort. The coda, in modulated harp-tones, came to a stop before a *fermata* which corresponded to those before mentioned, in order to cast anchor in the haven of the dominant, finishing with a witches'

Carl Tausig

dance of triplets doubled in thirds. This eighteen-page piece winds up with extreme *bravura*.

Tausig's left hand was a second right; he never appeared even to notice difficulties! Anton Rubinstein called him "the infallible;" Liszt spoke of his fingers as *brazen* ; Sérow said to me whenever we spoke of pianists: "Hear Tausig; you *must* hear Tausig!"

His distinguishing characteristic was, that he never played for *effect*, but was always absorbed in the piece itself and its artistic interpretation. This objectivity the general public never understood; whenever serpents are strangled, it always wants to know just how big and dangerous they are, and judges of this by the performer's behavior. The general public thinks that whatever *appears* easily surmounted, is not really difficult, and that son or daughter at home might do it just as well! But it was this outward calm, this perfect steadiness of Tausig's attitude, which crowned his virtuosity.

Well might he say, as I once heard him: "I am no drawing-room pianist, it is only in public that I can command all my resources!" Eccentric gestures, and playing with all one's limbs, may be, and are, very effective with the public; but such elements are inimical to art. Tausig's playing was flawlessly moulded.—Tausig would have charmed Chopin, whose perfect ease in overcoming mechanical difficulties he possessed, though paired with far superior strength and power.

Before I left Berlin, I discussed with Tausig Liszt's Fantasia on the *Don Juan* motive, which calls for the highest powers of the piano-virtuoso. Tausig said, with noble modesty: "For a long time I could not conquer this piece; not until I had returned to Bach and the last Beethoven Sonatas, and studied them again and again, would it surrender to me. You raise no objection to my interpretation of the *Don Juan* Fantasia? Well, I tell myself that I have not yet conquered the difficulties, I have only attacked them. He only is superior to them—only *He!* This is the secret of the impression *He* makes! You said in your French book: 'He is the Paganini of the piano'; that is true, and it pleased him, but it says far too little. Liszt exhibits in himself an absolute mastery over the entire realm of musical art, he is a predestined composer in the largest forms—in all! Out of his great diversity of gifts, arises his virtuosity; Paganini never soared as high as Liszt, he stopped at virtuosity!"

In fact, Liszt's piano-technique has been understood

Carl Tausig

as a spiritualized technique, a thing apart;—as a new train of ideas, as a thread spun on from Bach and Beethoven to us, reaching to the compositions of Liszt, as to the latest expression of the possibilities of the piano!

The great piano-virtuosos of the century may be compared with continents and countries.

Liszt, Chopin, and Henselt are continents; Tausig, Rubinstein, and Bülow are countries.

Thalberg was only the correct "gentleman-rider" of the piano, during the forty years which seem to lie a whole century behind our days! A rider, no matter how well he sits his horse, must get off sometimes! Thalberg rode perpetually. He called it *Fantaisie*— the one on *Moses*, for instance; he made music, like the trumpeter in Kaufmann's Museum in Dresden— blown through the air, not through the soul. Thalberg was the well-groomed piano; who saddles a note of his now-a-days? Only one of his lucubrations has musical promise—and that only in the beginning, the trot—his second *Caprice* (E flat major), in which the motive is charmingly bridled, and, at the end of the interminable *performance* (as the English call musical productions), sets off on a steeplechase and clears the fence in octave-leaps of two octaves!

Great Piano Virtuosos

Thalberg said that he would undertake to play side by side with Liszt, but that Liszt must sit behind a screen, and must not be seen while he was at it! Just there, and for the first time, Thalberg would have been thrown, for Liszt's soul would not have stayed behind the screen! "You resemble the spirit which you comprehend, not me!" Liszt might have told him.

Thalberg was a finished man of the world at the piano; the thumb of his right hand was his groom, whom he had elevated to the exalted position of conductor of the melody! The shifting of the accompaniment to the middle range of the piano was *not* the invention of Thalberg, but was introduced by Beethoven[16] in his first *Piano-concerto in C major*, Op. 15, Largo, which appeared in 1801; then again by Weber in the Andante of his *D minor Sonata*, in his *Invitation*, and in the Rondo of his *E flat major Concerto*.

An oft-spoken opinion is to the effect, that the piano has reached its climax in Liszt and Chopin.

Every period has its *raison d'être;* virtuosity had hers, and Tausig is the best evidence of this fact. It is the same with creative work. Life being divided between Church and Theatre—between the things

Carl Tausig

symbolized by these factors—the representatives of these "stages" on the piano are, foremostly, Beethoven and Weber.

Weber's sympathy was with life in general, Chopin's with the life of the higher classes of society in particular. Chopin did not feel less deeply than Weber, because he *felt* in Paris; but Chopin's sympathy was special, while Weber's was general—he sprang from *German* soil! There is no trace of opera or symphony in Chopin's music, while these elements haunt Weber's piano-music like the fantastic will-o'-the-wisps in the *Wolfsschlucht*. Chopin is always pure pianoforte, with a masterly pianistic treatment and piano-style superior to Weber; *Chopin* commands *all* technical resources, which Weber never mastered to an equal degree.

The relation of Chopin to Beethoven and Weber on the piano, is that of a peer to these great men. Beethoven's piano-music is to be regarded in the light of cartoons for orchestra and quartets, just as Kaulbach's cartoons in the Cathedral at Berlin are to be understood as paintings. Beethoven, as the incarnate Genius of the symphony, is always symphonic, both in his piano-concertos and in his violin-concertos. His thoughts, in their flight, leave the piano, never to return—they are lost in the infinitude of the Idea!

Even his quartets are abbreviated symphonies, despite their quartet-like equipment.

Tausig understood how to discriminate in Beethoven, as well as in Weber, at the piano. He played Beethoven's *A major Sonata*, Op. 101, with the most charming piano-coloring; the powerful Orchestra Fantasia in the *F minor Sonata*, Op. 57—which is called *appassionata* (as though all Beethoven's Sonatas were not *appassionate!*)—he performed orchestrally. He gave the *A flat major Sonata* with Pompeian coloring; and the last Sonata, Op. 111, was *colossal!*

Nothing is more important to the virtuoso than a proper comprehension of the tone-poet whom he undertakes to interpret. In this relation Tausig's lofty general education stood him in good stead, and his fine taste, largely the result of scientific research, in all things.

One may say what one will, but as an authoritative musical critic, Tausig takes an exceptional position; our great master Liszt will, for all time, be taken as the highest standard of musical criticism.

Before I speak of my meeting with Tausig in St. Petersburg, I must relate one more reminiscence

Carl Tausig

of Berlin, of that late autumn of 1868, ever-memorable by reason of the artist's genial kindliness.

Once when we were quite alone, Tausig made me sit at his piano, and said: "Play the highest part of this; the piece *cannot* be known to you."

It was a set of short, expressive compositions for four hands, by Schumann.

"There, you played that exactly as *He* would!"

I looked up at him, confused; on the one hand, I could not suppose that he was quizzing me; on the other, I appeared very foolish to myself.

"I am in earnest," he continued, "I repeat it, you played it just as *He* would!"

"But there is nothing to *play*, only to *understand*."

"That is just it—one does not teach *that* to one's lady-pupils! It quite astonished me; those are the *Journeys*—your foot-tours in Switzerland!" (He was still humorous in 1868; when I saw him in St. Petersburg, in 1870, that phase of his character had quite disappeared.) In a few days I appeared with two books of music in my hand.

"Ah," said he, "now you are going to take revenge for my examination; yes, I admit that it was an examination. I wished to see—never mind, tell me in what *I* am to be examined?"

Great Piano Virtuosos

"You see: '*Sonates progressives et agréables.*'" Tausig laughed most heartily and asked: "What is that to us?"

"To give pleasure," was my answer; "these are little operas in disguise, by Weber; just play the bass and listen attentively. The original is for piano and violin; this arrangement is by Czerny—as Cranz, the publisher in Hamburg, told me when I went to see him about it. Sonate 1, *rectius* Sonatine, F major, Allegro; *Before the Gate, Whitsuntide;* Larghetto; *Grandmother's Story at the Fireplace*, B major; Rondo, *amabile*, F major, *The Posthorn*. There is nothing of all this in the music, but I will bring it out," I said, confidently.

Tausig: "Let us begin with the fireplace."

"Yes! That is really very interesting! Once more! (begged Tausig) you seem to know it very well."

"Twenty years of faithful wedlock!"

"And still in love? Well, let us go before the Gate," laughed Tausig. "Also very interesting," he admitted. "But the Amabile, the Posthorn story, is nothing!"

"But the little eight-measure *minore?*" I asked.

"Yes! That is by a master again!"

"Sonate 2, Moderato, carattere espagnuolo, G major, *A German in Seville*. Adagio, C minor, *From*

Carl Tausig

a lost Opera, Didone abbandonata; Rondo, G major; Polish Air, *In the country, St. John's Day.*"

Tausig remarked: "*This* Spain might be in Germany!"

"Just like the Spain in *Don Giovanni*, I think."

"You think so? H'm, h'm! Well, perhaps! Adagio, interesting; Rondo, charming, modulation to B flat, into the lower dominant (C major), delicious—now the Rondo again—Oho, how abruptly the thing closes!"

"Sonate 3, Air russe, D minor, *The truth about Russia, unknown in Germany*, (how ingenuously Tausig glanced at me!). Maggiore, charming; see, I have written over it 'amoroso' (he smiled so kindly); Rondo, Presto, six-eight, D major, *Dance of the Elves*, charming beyond description."

"Let us have the Elves, then," urged Tausig.

"Yes, see there! That is a serious matter! The Rondo is very beautiful," said Tausig joyously, "and how abrupt at the close! That must be true! Now the Rondo over again!" he commanded.

"Notice the festoons of flowers from the thirteenth measure on! Another seduction of *Hüon;* but I must beg you to play the *primo* now, because I do the scales so badly."

Great Piano Virtuosos

"There is one in the bass that is more important, the whole orchestra enters there; I have not neglected my part — I shall stay below!" answered Tausig.

We played the Rondo three times. It is not long, only eighty-four measures altogether, — yet how much there is in it! "*An unmortgaged country-seat, with elves!*"

"Will you not have the rest — ?"

"Yes, I want the rest of it at once," urged Tausig.

"Sonate 4, E flat major, *Sunday, Game of Skittles. Sunflowers by the bowling-alley*. What fine, honest folk these be, we find in measure nine and the following. Rondo vivace, modestly illuminated garden, but still —"

Tausig: "But still! How charmingly he accented the idea, 'beloved brethren!'"

"Sonate 5, *In the theatre*. A major, Andante *con moto*, theme from the opera *Sylvana*, four-four."

Tausig: "Well now, are you ready?"

"Very! — Do you know what that is? Weber must have loved this theme; he worked it into variations for solo clarinet accompanied by almost solo pianoforte; that set is Op. 33, in B major; this set, in A, is Op. 10; there are more of the clarinet-variations; which is the earlier work?"

"*Darüber streiten die Städte*" [When doctors dis-

Carl Tausig

agree], aptly quoted Tausig; "according to all good methodology, the completer work is the last, I think." "Yes, but in our Op. 10 we have this devilish march-variation, Marcia Maestoso; only the most finished master could write that! The *Finale siciliano* is also charming!"

Tausig: "This No. 5 is really too pretty! Do you know, I have an idea! One could arrange these things as a Weber Fantasia, for drawing-room purposes. I shall do it sometime!" (A thought which should be utilized; one *must* love Weber; Rubinstein loved him!)

"The 6th Sonatalet is insignificant, the closing Polonaise is weak, but there's a pretty violoncello solo, or would you call it a bassoon?"

Tausig: "I should say *cornet à pistons!*" So *scherzoso* was he!

So we passed every day—unfortunately but six weeks! Two years passed; the news that, before Easter, Tausig was coming for a concert-season, raised the greatest interest in the compact group which formed the musical contingent of St. Petersburg. It was in March, 1870. I went directly to Tausig in the Hotel Demuth, where he was staying. He greeted me kindly, but I saw that he was a changed man. A cloud lay on his features; he was no longer cheerful! "You forgive me, as I see," he said, tactfully, "because I did not go to you—I make no visits; I leave the hotel only to go to my concerts, and then not until everything is quite ready and I can seat myself at the piano, as soon as I arrive." He handed me a cigar. "They are *the same!*" he said, with a sorrowful smile. I talked directly of indifferent matters—it seemed the best course to pursue, although I was not yet certain of the reason. He must have thought so, too, as he rose quickly and said: "I must play you your *Invitation.*" He played only the passage to which, in his arrangement of the piece, is added a *motu contrario* for the left hand. I was fairly astonished at this virtuosity soaring freely, as it were, into space, even in a domain where I felt so thoroughly at home!—

"If it amuses you," he said, "I can do it faster."

This time he played the double passage *pp*, in a fabulous prestissimo tempo, smiled, and rose.

This delivery was not natural, it was *scurrilous*, as Master Hoffmann (Kreissler) was wont to say. The artist must have been grieving! At my request, however, he played me the entire piece with his Arabesques (the distinguishing title of his arrangement).

Carl Tausig

The *Invitation*, one of the most widely known pieces of the piano-repertory, was written by Weber some fifty years ago, yet it is still young! I consider it the most significant, and the most gratifying piece in rondo-form without accompaniment, that we possess. This tender, yet so remarkably brilliant inspiration, is meant for an intimate piano-piece, and finds its natural place in the family circle and the drawing-room. If it is to appear before an audience of two thousand people, of course it must don ball-attire and appear in the full panoply of the modern, Olympic concert-grand, an instrument which reaches far beyond the possibilities of the piano known to Weber. Thus Tausig treated the *Aufforderung* in his variant. The rocking *cantilena* (so aptly denoted by Weber), to which, in the original, the accompaniment is played in the middle of the piano, was placed by Tausig in the medium as a bass voice — that proper to a dancer declaring his love to his partner—quite as an *a parte*—while in Weber's arrangement this charming *cantilena* is more representative of the whole scene.

To me, the most artistic part of Tausig's interpretation of the *Aufforderung* was the *Minore*, to which he gave a well-nigh boisterous effect.

Great Piano Virtuosos

I told him so. His answer was: "It is pleasant that you should praise my reading throughout, when all your life you have played it differently! Shall you write about it?"

"Certainly! about your Arabesques in the *Invitation*, I will write just what I now tell you. Personally, and for the best of reasons, *I* shall remain faithful to my Weber text."

He laughed in the old manner. "Yes, it is *devilish hard!* see, here, where the *motus contrarius* in the passage touches minor, and yet the polished floor of the ball-room must remain as smooth and mirror-like as ever! I have often thought of you, when I played it—but I shall play it much better this evening; my wings grow when I play in public. You will see. And now, good-bye—and, like a good fellow, don't come here again, for I have become an insupportable companion!" There was a touch of his old Berlin humor!

I always go early to concerts and opera on special occasions. I like to see the tribe of double-basses gradually stretch out their long necks; to see the wind-players fumble in their cases; to see trumpets and kettle-drums making ready; the violins in conference! What thoughts arise the while! There is

Carl Tausig

something grand about an orchestra! It is the *Dœmos*, whence everything proceeds, and whither everything returns; that is the cosmic idea, and the orchestra is the Church of Instrumentalism.

Such an important fraction of the civilized populace should never be invited to an improvised meal, but only to a symposium!

This time Beethoven's *E flat major Concerto* was on the programme—a worthy banquet!

The fate that compels the traveller (for in large cities one always *travels)* brought me there one hour before the time. The vast interior of the Hall of the Nobles in St. Petersburg *(Dvorœnskoje Sobranie)* usually resembles a dimly lighted crypt, at such times. The hall itself was but half-lit, but already completely filled. I had not seen such a sight for forty years! I hastened to the artists' room in order to tell Tausig about it; he was not there, however, and appeared at each concert only just in time to play.

This hall has, for the past forty years, been the official meeting-place of the nobility, and is one of the most beautiful—if not the most beautiful—in Europe. The roof is supported on either side by rows of twelve Corinthian columns of polished white

Great Piano Virtuosos

stucco, in two stories (with gallery); there are three pillared doorways at each end, through which one descends into the hall by a few steps. Between the pillars hang twenty-eight great chandeliers; from the ceiling hang eight more, of colossal size. Of course the acoustics, amid such surroundings, are not all that could be desired, but they are good, nevertheless. The hall is frequently used for festivals, balls, and court ceremonies. The orchestra-platform is built out into the hall.

With this orchestra have appeared all the great musicians of Europe. Here: Franz Liszt! Here, the great singers: Pasta, Viardot, Sontag (Countess Rossi). Here: Vieuxtemps, Ernst, Sivori, Ole Bull. Here sang Rubini! Here took place *all* the grand functions of musical life in St. Petersburg; while the two Counts Wielhorski were leaders in taste, tendency, and a right appreciation, by virtue of their artistic superiority—morally, not by force, and hence with the more enduring results; for these two patrons and artists, unique in the musical annals of Europe, never occupied an official station in music. Their followers were drawn to them *organically*, by *natural selection*.

Rubinstein, who belonged to this great musical pe-

Carl Tausig

riod, once said to me: "In these days, everything is open to the public!"

"Dat *vincla* libertas," said I to myself.

In any event, public spirit ought to rise to that level, which marked the leadership of those eminent minds—a leadership effective from internal reasons.

At Tausig's concerts every seat in these rooms was taken; even the balcony, facing the Emperor's box, and belonging to the diplomatic corps, was given up to the public. The gallery at the capitals was a compact mass of men and women; in the entrances, between the windows and the pillars, stood row upon row of closely packed people, the last row even standing upon the window-ledges!

Thus was Tausig received! In keeping with the artist's modest manner of presenting himself, the entrance-prices were also modest, yet, according to German rates, they were high. They ranged from one ruble[17] (gallery) as high as two, three, and five, for the reserved seats. On the morning of the first concert, Tausig's secretary had already sold three thousand rubles' worth of tickets. The gross proceeds amounted to double that sum, and all three concerts were equally thronged. It was the same in Moscow, where all the tickets were sold before the

Great Piano Virtuosos

arrival of the artist. Yet, after his return from Moscow to St. Petersburg, he could not be induced to give one more concert.

Well, Tausig appeared upon the platform, and seated himself before the piano, which he had brought from Berlin. He was greeted with a storm of applause, such as an artist returning home after long absence, might scarcely hope to receive.

Now the *E flat major Concerto* struck up!

The artist was wholly oblivious of self—I saw it instantly—that he might fully recognize the sway of his imperial mistress, Art, in one of her noblest works!

His club-strokes, meeting the onset of the orchestra, were fearful! These were his answers to the rigors of life, as they affect the artistic soul!

Tausig played the Concerto by heart, as he played all his programmes. He was a rhapsodist, drunk with the passion of the immortal poet! The passages were like toys in his grasp! I never heard a more fiery, a more manly exposition of the flame of the Rondo.

And how uniquely this Rondo rushed into the hall! In the delicate second theme Tausig seemed to say: "It is nothing to me now! all is over!"

Carl Tausig

In the leaps in C (in the modulation) which were like electric sparks, he said: "*This* is I!" It was the epitome of delicacy, the most perfect elegance. I thought of what he had said in Berlin: "That concerto is my *specialty*."

He played up to that programme of the work which the press (*Kölnische Zeitung*, 1871), at the time of the secular celebration at Bonn, expressed far better than I could do:[18]

"This Concerto is a truly noble tone-poem! All it requires, in order to appear in the full splendor of its steel panoply, is a knightly player,—not one who would strip off its armor, and take away its weapons, to bring it forth clothed in a silken jacket and soft shoes!" Tausig was this knightly player in St. Petersburg, and the place of honor could scarce have been wrested from him in Bonn! There he would have played *pro Germania!*

His solo playing in St. Petersburg extended over the entire répertoire: from Bach and Scarlatti to Mozart and Beethoven; from Field to Chopin; through Weber and Schumann, to Liszt. All styles were simple, to him; he united in himself the characteristics of the most diverse natures!

Let us sum up the attributes of the artist now torn

Great Piano Virtuosos

from our midst: His command of all musical resources was so great, that in this command resided the poetry of a conqueror holding sovereign sway over material and machinery,—a poetry peculiar and apart. His talent for the strict style (fugue, the imitative style) was unique. He played fugues, and the like, with the charm of the most charming treatment of the free style; as was once said of him: His neatness in every part, the *nuances* of his touch, made this domain popular, generally intelligible, universally interesting. In the fugue we confront the *letter*, into which we are to breathe the *spirit* of Art, not a subjective personality; an artistic subjectivity, in a narrow sense. Tausig possessed, in a high degree, the power of subordinating his own nature to the necessity of his art, so that in the fugue he was peculiarly at home. He commanded the entire arsenal of the utmost possibilities of the piano as expressed in the compositions of Liszt, and was a finished interpreter of Chopin.

In a word, he was one of the most prominent virtuosos the world has ever known, an *infaillibler triumphator* at the piano.

Have, anima pia! Te! amicissimum sodalem———moriturus salutat!

Adolph Henselt

*Erlösung der Sinnlich-
keit durch das Ideal*

Adolph Henselt

ARTHUR SCHOPENHAUER, who apprehends the world, in his philosophy, as Will and Conception, once said: "The greatest good fortune is never to have been born."

Never to have written may also be regarded as a fairly acceptable piece of good fortune! The difficulty of writing is, that you must not only talk — you must say something; by writing you always make more enemies than friends, and your gain is but a symbol!

In the *Berliner Musikzeitung*, Nos. 37–39, 1868, appeared a series of articles comprising Liszt, Chopin, and Tausig, and holding out a promise of a continuation, more especially because a halt was made before the most unique phenomenon of this century on the keyboard — Adolph Henselt. If we speak of Henselt as the most unique phenomenon on the keyboard, we now have to justify this designation by means of internal evidence.

In absolute power over *every* resource of the piano, and, therefore, over *every* style, Liszt is to be understood as *cosmic* — i. e., universal. Tausig, who treated the apparatus, the medium, as an art in itself, leaned thereby more towards universality, than individuality. Chopin was too individual in production, to be able to express his entire individuality in reproduction, as an artist deficient in physical command of the medium. We say, his *entire* individuality; for in details of interpretation, in a *natural* elegance all his own—springing from feeling, not artificial—in the taste and fervency of all his conceptions, the pianist Chopin likewise discovered incomparable individuality of its kind,—a Polish (Sarmatian) individuality with French breeding, French manners, with the advantages and disadvantages of both nationalities.

By reason of his lack of physical power, he composed everything in song-style; every detail of his work conforms to this style—in this art he was a pastel-painter, "*wie noch Keiner war*." His Mazurkas are the journal of his spiritual journeys into the socio-political domain of the Sarmatian dreamworld! There his powers of reproduction were at home, there dwelt the individuality of Chopin the pianist. He represented his *dream-land*, Poland, in the Parisian *salons*, and even dared, in the time of Louis Philippe, to predict for his beloved country a far-reaching political independence. Chopin was

Adolph Henselt

the *only political* pianist. He interpreted Poland, he *composed* Poland!

French life, the French schools of Art and Science in general, were not altogether without influence on Franz Liszt. This was shown at the time by the fact, that this great *apparition* at the pianoforte, the greatest phenomenon ever known on the pianoforte,—that Liszt placed in the front rank the attainments of a mechanical skill not wholly free from a certain stereotyped formalism—French precision acting along conventional lines—and brought its influence to bear on conventionalism and on all things "that the Fashion sternly parts," as the poet [19] has it. His style was at that time sufficient unto itself, much as the French language is self-sufficing. The artist's genius, his "immortal part," freed him from French influences, and drew him ever closer to Germany, the collective fatherland of musical art—an advantage which obtained for him equal mastery over all other styles; by means of *German* intellect, from *German* depth, *German* knowledge and power, to enter at will into the soul-life of France and Italy.

Midway between Liszt and Chopin—*in a way*, the connecting-link between their contrasting natures—

stands Henselt, a primitive German phenomenon, a *Germania* at the piano. *Henselt* is *German* in everything, in production and in reproduction. *German* is, for us, synonymous with faithful, honest, real! All that is true and upright in the world, all that lies deep, all the deepest and noblest qualities which live in the human breast, may safely be called *German!* But Henselt is not only German, he is, in the best and broadest sense of the term, *student-German*; in his indestructible youthfulness of spirit, in his entire exemption from social and conventional constraint, both in art and life, in his Utopian views of life—the reality of which exists in the ideal! Student-life is a German institution which — like a happy island in the midst of the sea of ordinary society—symbolizes the youth of the world *(juventus mundi)*, as Gladstone said of Greece! This element is a token of true German feeling, and on these grounds we make an analogous application to Henselt.

Therefore, when we say that, against Liszt and Chopin, Henselt stands out as a *student-German* phenomenon "such as never was before," we obtain another key to a better understanding of his manner. Our aim is to discriminate, to characterize.

Adolph Henselt

Commonplaces of acknowledgment,—qualifications fitting similar phenomena, will not do; for by such means neither characteristic traits nor well-grounded comprehension can be realized; and these alone are available for criticism, because they establish facts.

In order to solve our problem we had to determine upon a standpoint from which to view Henselt. We found the *Germanic* standpoint. We shall, therefore, first submit a small, general portion of our observations; then describe the great artist by descriptions of some of his compositions (as with Weber and Chopin); and close with a sketch of the artist as a man. For the life of an artist is a totality which he can abandon only in episodes, and to which his best impulses must ever be true—if he be a genuine artist.

For the past thirty-two years [20] Henselt has lived in St. Petersburg, where he never appears in public. Twice every year he visits Germany, but even there he is heard only by a chosen few. Therefore it may be agreeable to German readers to hear about an artist who belongs to the artistic fame of the German fatherland in such a high degree, that if one dared calculate and classify, one might name Henselt as the only artist among the great pianists who

Great Piano Virtuosos

is Liszt's equal—although in the specifically subjective domain he belongs to a more specialized sphere. Henselt alone has, first of all, the same command over the resources, in fullness of tone and the same finish of execution; this execution is unapproachable—above all comparison *(omni exceptione major)*. We do not care for comparisons, however, but will criticise each of these phenomena apart, upon its own ground.

In his creation, in his style, in his entire personality Henselt is German, thoroughly German, without general polish. He has his own peculiar polish, his own peculiar finish; he is a law and an end unto himself. By this law he departs from the good old school, but arrives at very individual results. He was once a pupil of Hummel—that is, if one can speak of him as being any one's *pupil!* However, every one must *begin*, therefore it is necessary to mention that the foundation of Henselt's execution is a very solid one. We should call it *classic*, had not the term been so stupidly misused, were it not odious to us, and did we not rather confine its application to the Greek and Roman authors according as one or the other treats his mother-tongue well or ill. We shall call Henselt's mode of expression, taken as

Adolph Henselt

a whole, romantic—in feeling and spirit like Weber, whom he much resembles in disposition. Romanticism is a distinctly German propensity which is most prominently developed in Henselt. Even when the artist develops a lighter vein, proffers a modest drawing-room piece *(Liebeslied, Fontaine)*, and the ordinary listener discerns sentimentality, refined sensibility—there too, and in the smallest possible compass, is Henselt romantic in the same sense in which Weber is romantic in *Der Freischütz*, where even *Ännchen's* simple songs are flooded with moonlight for every one that has taste to appreciate them.

In his outward appearance the artist is also specifically German; in his dignified, simple carriage, in his self-poised manner combined with the sincerest modesty, because he never is or will be satisfied with his achievement—a fact which the keen observer easily recognizes, and only the vulgar misjudges. Henselt pursues an ideal of perfection, which never permits him a moment of unalloyed delight. Hence it comes that Henselt is the only artist to exhibit the phenomenon—remarkable, indeed, but grounded in his innermost nature—that immediately on finishing a given piece or movement, to the utmost astonishment and rapture of his chosen audience, he would play it over, and even over again, as though at the command of some higher power, quite unconscious of his surroundings! These were moments of supreme ecstasy, of entire isolation from the outer world—in which the man is no longer master of himself, in which the artistic soul alone is active; moments in which the artist approaches nearer to his ideal, which he longs with such passionate yearning to reach that the outer world, his own self, and the impression made upon his auditors, are quite forgotten! Had he, at such moments, had a suspicion of any audience, he would gladly have had them thrown out of the window! Such is the result of my observations of the past thirty-two years!

Such unconscious, rhapsodic *reprises* of this kind usually ran on in accelerated motion, with modifications of form, in a concentration of expression upon some darling passage which was to him *his* Rezia, *his* Agatha, to whom, over hill and dale, through fire and water, he works his way, that with his beloved he may sacrifice himself upon the altar of the purest enthusiasm! One does not experience mere enjoyment in hearing Henselt, one is intoxicated and elevated at the same moment. Another dis-

Adolph Henselt

tinctive trait in Henselt is that, in the midst of compositions—wherever his enthusiasm seizes him, when he soars towards his ideal, he doubles the singing melody that quite fills his heart, by humming it himself! The artist's voice is anything but lovely, and injures the effect, as he knows right well when he is told that he has been singing again; for he himself does not know it, or suspect it! *Never*, never have I heard such a magical *cantilena* flow from the pianoforte, as in those moments when Henselt's voice joined his playing! But even then *he* is never satisfied, he was never happy for even a moment. Never does Henselt say, or feel, or think, with the romantic poet:

> *Alle Wünsche, alle Träume*
> *Waren herrlich nun gestillt!*
> *Das Verlangen war erfüllt.*
> *Fröhlich rauschten grüne Bäume!* *

Henselt first appeared in St. Petersburg in the concert-season of 1838, and since then has left us only occasionally. I happened to be at Count Wielhorski's when Henselt first called there. I shall never forget the extraordinary impression he made by the interpretation of his *F sharp Major Étude*. It was

* *Kaiser Oktavianus.*

Great Piano Virtuosos

like an Æolian harp hidden beneath garlands of sweetest flowers! An intoxicating perfume was crushed from the blossoms under his hands—soft, like falling rose-leaves, the alternating sixths, which, in one and the same octave, pursued, teazed, embraced, and enraptured! Such a charm of rich fullness of tone in *pianissimo* had never before been heard on the piano! After the delicate whisper in the principal theme, the *Minore* entered energetically, mounting from one degree of power to another, taking the instrument by storm—to lose itself again in a magic dialogue in sixths! Thirty-two years have passed since then, but the enchanting picture still lives before the inner eye.

Henselt must have perceived how enraptured we were with his performance, for as soon as he had finished the piece, he commenced again at the most touching part of his poem, and played it through once again, with modified gradations of expression. It was like gleaning after a harvest of joy! He must have been satisfied with himself, and have rejoiced to read his instant triumph in the eyes of connoisseurs of such high standing as the Counts Wielhorski.

In quite a different style, flowing more quietly,

Adolph Henselt

broadly, and deeply, followed his *Poëme d'amour* in B major, which, passing over from an unquestionably new nocturne-style, changes to a not less deeply felt allegro in variation-style, and closes with the highest degree of bravura in arpeggios which covered the whole extent of the instrument — and which he hurled like heavy, well-aimed spears — without exceeding the limits of euphony, without once overstepping the measure of power allowed to the piano.

Such playing had never been heard! Such tenderness allied to so much force; a depth of meaning so sufficient to itself, with all its euphemistic concessions to the audience, was an artistic feat, a phenomenon, wholly unique.

The success of the concert given at the big theatre by Henselt, was so extraordinary, the result so great, towering above everything of the kind which had been known abroad, the victory over the old world of the piano so indisputable—that the artist acceded to the out-spoken wishes of the public, and brought his Penates from Germany to St. Petersburg. Henselt's coming to us marked the obsolescence of the Hummel-Field school, and brought the piano into quite another channel. A deep shadow fell over

Great Piano Virtuosos

the old literature, which was represented in St. Petersburg by Charles Mayer,[21] who in his way was a finished, swift-fingered, smooth, but very dry *pianiste-compositeur* — and by Reinhardt, who had studied with Field in Moscow, but resembled his master only in the outward part of piano ornamentation, not in the spirit of his interpretations. Mayer himself swore by Field, and posed as his best pupil; both these musicians understood little of Beethoven, nothing at all of Weber. Mayer had had the presumption to go over to Hummel, whose compositions passed for the highest kind of piano-music, in the twenties and thirties! Now, Hummel was but a starting-point for Henselt, through whose compositions, aside from their unparalleled interpretation by the author, a new era began: the era of lyric personality, subjective dramatic intention, plastic execution, bearing internal evidence of a real human right to be. This tendency, this new *salon*-literature, had its origin in the good old school and belonged, from a technical standpoint, to a straight guild; now, however, it had nothing more to do with schools and pedants, with pattern and routine, but turned its doctrinary ideas to account for humanity, in audience and adepts.

Adolph Henselt

Henselt's compositions seek to express emotion, and not speculative musical ideas; wherefore they should not be judged merely from reading, but must be played, or heard.

The abstract idea so powerful in Schumann, for example, is foreign to Henselt; but nowhere in his compositions do we find the voids which, in Hummel, hide behind passages and endless tinklings. Henselt paints pictures of deep feeling within small frames, and his mastery of the medium enables him — through polyphony in composition, through positions, stretches, and turning to account every possibility of the piano, to give interest to compositions in which the original idea was of slight value. It is the most fruitful treatment of the piano, *beyond which* Liszt and Chopin were able to pass only in details, not in essentials. It is, rather, the same domain occupied by the Olympian piano of our day, which dominates publicity, influences privacy, and cannot well lend itself to simplified expression; for such simplicity, to receive vitality of form, must be paired with a proportionally greater and more primitive creative gift—one on a par with the greatest masters of composition, ay! overpassing them, after the delirious revel of our days in outward effect! In

Great Piano Virtuosos

these days we seem to rely more upon form and outward appearance than on the deep musical production—the *idea*.

Time is generally the most righteous judge of worth. Henselt's compositions have held their own in the piano-repertory for forty years. That is saying a great deal; that is a proof that they embody living thought which must survive fashion and the influence of the auspicious moment—that they are, in a word, *vital thoughts*—which cannot be said of many of their contemporaries. It is not merely the fundamental expression of love-yearning, tempered by strong dash of romanticism, in Henselt's compositions, but, no whit less, their tragi-dramatic aim, which gives them value and importance. In the Études *Eroica* and *Dankgebet nach Sturm*, there is an amount of energy, earnestness, and a dramatic note, which, before his time, were not to be found on the piano. Henselt is, altogether, a phenomenon unexcelled by any other of our day; a phenomenon, in its place and period, of equal rank with Liszt, *i.e.*, overmastering, epoch-making in art. Henselt is not a music-spirit pure and simple, apart from the pianoforte; he is a spirit of *piano*-music—belonging essentially to the piano and indissolubly bound to

Adolph Henselt

it. Hence it is that Weber and Henselt are so much alike in spirit—that Weber is so much more sympathetic to the artist than Beethoven. Weber lives in the region of loving human souls, Beethoven's influence over the world is through the strength and power of speculative thought! These two aims are not opposed, they run parallel; they do not interfere with one another, they divide the world between them. Of Beethoven's three first piano-trios (Op. 1) Henselt said in his pithy way: "They *grew*, the later ones were made;" and the same, in a higher degree, he thought of the great thinker's solo sonatas, which form a cult by themselves, as every one knows.

I know that I lay myself open to contradiction here —it might be war to the knife, but for the fact that I shall never venture to argue with Henselt! His obstinacy and tenacity are too strong—*he* would never yield! He sits walled in by his own convictions, walled in with the precepts of his good old school—even though these precepts are no longer impregnable, or enlightened by the general latter-day art-philosophy. But one example is worth mentioning. Beethoven, in the finale of the choral symphony, uses the chord of the seventh on f in D

Great Piano Virtuosos

minor, with the minor ninth *(b)*, and the full dominant harmony *(a, c sharp, e, g)*, whereby the entire diatonic minor scale of D is heard at once. At a dinner in St. Petersburg, which Henselt gave in honor of Berlioz, the latter spoke of this chord as a "monster" which he could not understand. Henselt rose from the table, opened a piano and seated himself—not without some irritation—on the keys, with the words: "It sounds something like this!"[22]

Henselt says that Bach can never grow old—and that is very true; but the reason lies in the nature of the fugue as a conventional form, not in the superiority of the thought. Such a study of Bach as Henselt made, every day of his life, has never before been heard of! He played the fugues most diligently on a piano so muffled with feather quills that the only sound heard was the dry beat of the hammers against the muffled strings; it was like the bones of a skeleton rattled by the wind! In this manner the artist spared his ears and his nerves, for he reads, at the same time, on the music-rack, a very thick, good book—the Bible—truly the most appropriate companion for Bach. After he has played Bach and the Bible quite through, he begins over again. The few people whom Henselt allows to approach him in

Adolph Henselt

those late hallowed evening hours, he requests to continue their conversation,—that does not disturb him in the least;—but the rattle of the skeleton in the piano disturbs *them*, and tortures their nerves instead of quieting them. Seated at a dumb piano with Bach and the Bible for company, the composer of many love-songs, of the *Poëme d'amour*, the most keen-eared tone-reveller among virtuosi, earned his daily artistic bread! One might meditate much on this; it is a long leap—a *salto mortale*—from the Prophets to Theocritus and Tibullus!

Such a strange phenomenon is this artist!—and in these traits, to which much might be added, he is, so to speak, a second Faust-Wagner: "In truth I know much, but I would know all," without contradicting his genuine artist-nature, but confirming it in genuine German fashion.

The effect Henselt produced in St. Petersburg was so great, that he became all at once the all-engrossing topic of conversation at the pianoforte; he concentrated, in his own person, the function of instructor in all the most influential circles and at Court, where the Empress immediately appointed him Court Pianist. He kept open house, gave no more concerts, and limited his consuming activity to composition and to teaching — his lessons he managed with almost unheard-of punctuality and energy.

His *Piano Concerto in F minor* dates from this time; we should call it the last possible *three-part* Concerto;—also his Trio in A minor, which, by reason of the contemporary movement, stands in the constellation of Mendelssohn.

In order to hear Henselt, one had either to become his pupil, which was not easy, or to belong to his circle of intimate acquaintances—which was still more difficult. To the latter he played, as he said, on Sunday mornings in winter for several hours, occasions of most solemn gatherings of the faithful. These *matinées* at Henselt's, as they were called, were most extraordinary; the artist played one piece after another without halt or rest,—often without any interruption. He thought little about his audience, unless the foremost beauties of the city happened to be present. He appeared to regard the performance in the light of exercises of a loftier scope—*coram populo*—for he was always playing exercises; for years he always had a dumb piano on his knees, on which he uninterruptedly punished his fingers, in company or by himself—for instance, at

Adolph Henselt

his concerts between each two numbers. I shall never forget how—a few minutes after one of his most brilliant triumphs at a concert in the Hall of the Nobility—I went to the artists' room with Count Wielhorski to speak with Henselt, and found him, surrounded by the flood-tide of a concert-evening, busy with his dumb piano! There was something in this of Hoffmann's *Kreissler*—it was the artist's confession of faith, his way of giving himself up entirely to his art, to the exclusion of every other interest. I have often regretted it for his sake, but have always understood it as a rare *faithfulness* to conviction, as an exaggeration of the *sense of duty* to his life-work for art,—as a proof of endurance and strength of character such as is peculiar only to the Germanic nature. This was not understood by every one, however—this longing of Henselt's to grasp with his hands the ever-receding horizon of ideal perfection!

Not less significant of his character is the fact that the mere thought of giving a concert makes him ill; after his first appearance, no amount of persuasion was sufficient to induce him to give another concert —in thirty-three years he gave but three! And a speculator offered to pay him in advance the highest

Great Piano Virtuosos

price he could reasonably demand if without any further trouble he would only sit down at the piano and play, the speculator taking whatever remained of the receipts over and above the price which he should see fit to demand;—but Henselt absolutely refused.

It is quite as impossible to induce him to attend a concert given by another, or the opera; he devotes himself entirely to his art, to his scholars, to the Court, to Bach and the Bible. Before Bach comes, however, he still pursues his course of bodily health-gymnastics every evening; forcing, in the sweat of his brow, and in spite of every fatigue and all opposition, his hands and feet to perform all sorts of difficult evolutions on a horizontal bar! He had once got a notion that it was beneficial, and Henselt never changes his opinion. These gymnastics of his have a not uninteresting point of departure.

In the days of Emperor Nicholas hygienic gymnastics came into fashion through the performances of a Swedish gymnast whose influence reached the highest social circles. For several winters the Emperor visited, early each morning, the *manége* in the palace of the Prince of Oldenburg, where he, in company with the Grand Duke, the Prince, and the

Adolph Henselt

Duke of Leuchtenberg, practised gymnastics. In this Henselt, as a friend of royalty, took part. Many years have passed since then, and of all who met there Henselt alone continues the exercises—a striking example of the persistence of the German nature. For the same hygienic reasons, the artist walks endless distances every day in St. Petersburg, sometimes letting his carriage accompany him, but oftener preferring to do without it.

Henselt is General Inspector of the music-classes in the royal educational institutions in St. Petersburg and Moscow which are under the management of the Prince of Oldenburg. In dark winter evenings Henselt walks quite alone from the Smolna Monastery—one of the largest—through a peculiarly lonely part of the town back to his own house. No remonstrance has any effect. We told him he might be waylaid. "That would not be easy," was his only answer. "I am agile, I do gymnastics—and I have this life-preserver!" pointing to his stick. So it will always be; for a yielding Henselt, at any age, is unimaginable.—In those institutions Henselt teaches whole generations of well-trained instructresses, thus assuring generations a respectable livelihood for which they have not ceased to be grateful.

Great Piano Virtuosos

Henselt's great Études are to be considered as poems, "Songs without Words," and he would surely have named them so had this title, brought into vogue by Mendelssohn, not already appeared. The expression *Étude* is not in this case to be understood —as are Cramer's—in the sense of exercises for piano-instruction. Everything in life is *study*, practice; we shall never reach the end of practising and learning! But *these* inspirations [Henselt's Études] assume previously finished study; they are of the first rank in the mass of literature which has appeared under the title of Études, in which Chopin culminates.

Henselt's Études are not inferior to those of Chopin, but present an essentially different emotional realm; they move in a different social sphere, with different forms of intercourse. If we seek to comprehend these differences, we shall fathom the character of both artist-natures and shall discover another criterion for a proper estimate of Henselt.

Henselt, in common with Chopin, acts with *direct* effect; the effect which speculative musical thought does not need, and which is most effective on the piano. He shares with Chopin the peculiarity of directing the whole power of the apparatus to the

Adolph Henselt

sense of hearing. Henselt differs from Chopin as the former higher French society, as the *salon*, in a word, differs from German society and civilization. During the past few years Paris has become altogether demoralized, becoming a sort of robber-romance. As early as the days of Louis Philippe, the scene of Dumas' novels was laid in Paris. The Parisian *salon* of yore exists now only in the literature of the time, in its music, in Chopin. Take up a novel of Balzac; you will find forms of intercourse, relations, feminine characters and personalities, which make up a world apart, having no slight power of attraction, but unable to lay claim to ideality. *Béatrix*, in *Les Amours forcés*, by Balzac (not to mention his imitators), may serve as a type. It is precisely *so* with Chopin. Not so much *what* he says, as *how* he says it, is the *punctum saliens*—the main point. Whatever seems *correct* to Parisians, and is accepted by Parisians, must have universal vitality, and a frivolous conception of the mutual relation of the sexes plays the leading rôle. A more fervent feeling, a deeper conception, is not precluded, but disappears beneath the conventional purple cover under which this very exclusive society seeks to prolong its artistic existence.

Great Piano Virtuosos

On the other hand, take a novel by Auerbach, Spielhagen, or any of our best German authors. Perhaps you will not find such accomplished people as occupy the French scene, and the forms of intercourse will not prove so charming; the language will hardly be modelled on the patterns which receive French sanction; but the characters will belong to ideality, a loftier expression of life, and not to a material point of view masquerading in the venal draperies of the latest fashion. It is just *so* with Henselt, who reaches his ideal from life itself—a true German procedure. Chopin and the French exalt a life, justified solely by convention and example, to an ideal in which they live, and for this reason recognize therein their own artistic justification! This tendency is unwholesome, pathological. However great the charm which its procedures possess, when all is told it is but a poisoning with refined poisons, a poisoning, let us say, by burning perfumed tapers, whose *flame* alone is an emblem of real life!

This refined and effeminate character of modern French literature—which is reflected, as it were, in Chopin, finds exceptions in his *Polonaises*, which are (for him) the higher, more objective form (his *Odes*), and his *Ballades*, which are pictures in small frames

Adolph Henselt

(Sonnets—to which his Nocturnes, *especially*, belong). Such exceptions in no wise alter the character of the phenomenon as a whole; one can find depths, and genuine pearls, even in Balzac and his epigones.

Not unconditionally, not without reservations, do we classify either phenomenon as *higher* than the other; we would only *discriminate*.

H. von Grimm[23] called Chopin a *Weltschmerzler*. Chopin may pass for a lyric epicure; any depreciative epithets are out of place where a noble spirit like Chopin is concerned, who, like Balzac, like all those Parisian exotics, moved in a self-constructed, self-imagined *milieu* (as they were wont to say), yet still bore the unmistakable mark of genius.

Chopin is, with few exceptions, a charming watercolor painter; Henselt paints *al fresco* even when his subject appears to exclude the broader style.

In the difference of their natures, in the irreconcilable divergence between French and German civilization *(quia æterna inter ea est pugna!)*, lies the natural reason why Henselt does not play Chopin as that master ought to be played; and we can but agree with the great virtuoso, that, when one is a Henselt, one has a right to play as one likes, as we once heard him remark.

Great Piano Virtuosos

We spoke of Henselt's interpretation of Chopin, only because the question: "How do you understand Chopin?" is one of the gravest one can put to a representative of the modern piano. In Henselt's interpretation of the Mazurkas and the Nocturnes Chopin (and I say it from my personal acquaintance with this rare nature) would have felt as little at home as would a Parisian in the midst of German society, because a certain free-and-easy manner is found in this society even in its highest circles, and may be ascribed to the effect of German university life, which permeates and influences all grades of German social life.

Henselt's magnificently powerful art of playing showed to advantage in Chopin's ornamental pieces —which are in Pompeian, not colossal style, and therefore refractory to a Titanic conception. With a certain pleasurable consciousness of strength confronted with weakness, Henselt lets the *time* take the leading part in the Mazurkas; he uses his heavy brush for fullness of tone, where the whole fabric is crocheted and woven; his *rubato* is not the Chopin *rubato*, it is a shifting of the tempo, not a general dislocation of the visual angle for the phenomenon as a whole, like the effect of a scene viewed through

Adolph Henselt

the small end of an opera-glass. How I should have enjoyed witnessing Chopin's ecstasy, could he have heard Henselt! have heard him whisper, lighten, thunder through his A minor Étude!—This rendering of Chopin by Henselt is so extraordinary, so indescribably grand, so deeply poetic, so infinitely idealized, as if by Oberon's wand, that I cannot find words to depict it. One finds no trace, in reading, of these never-resting figures flowing from diminished harmonies; from the delicate *melismata* and the ineffable tones produced by the right hand to the herculean strokes of the left, by Henselt, they are like the twinkling of stars, the unknown language of the heights.

"*Himmelhoch jauchzend, zu Tode betrübt!*"
Herein lies the immeasurable superiority of the German over the Italian nature! Taken all in all, this performance of Henselt's is one of the grandest on the pianoforte, as such, that it has ever been my privilege to hear. From his soul the artist loves this poem, for years he has fostered and tended it, and warmed it on his breast; when Henselt plays the A minor Étude, he plays it again and again, for he cannot satiate himself with the euphony, with whose atmosphere he surrounds himself! If there

Great Piano Virtuosos

is any one performance in which the artist's consuming impulse for perfection was realized I believe it is this—and my opinion is the result of years of observation.

Some of Henselt's principal compositions are his *Concerto in F minor* and the great *Duo* in a movement for piano and horn, in B minor. The Concerto is the climax of the most brilliant concert-*bravura*, allied, however, to a good musical content. What one might be tempted to regard as passage-work, is solid thought in figurate style; but the execution is so difficult, that the artist was never satisfied with his own rendering, and never publicly played the work in St. Petersburg. Neither was he ever quite satisfied with an accompaniment. He often played the *Concerto* at his own home, and such a colossal subjection of the greatest difficulties (difficulties which have, however, a purpose) laid claim to the greatest musical interest. The *Duo* likewise required a master-pianist to interpret it. In our opinion it is the most interesting in this entire literature, as an exponent of pianoforte-*bravura* in combination with a second instrument, with a scope gratifying to the interest in the idea. *Neither* of these works is as widely known, as it deserves to be—but this is not

Adolph Henselt

caused by their technical difficulties alone; his residence being so far removed from Germany, and his strong objection to publicity, may have had something to do with it. Hans von Bülow played the *Concerto* in St. Petersburg, and esteemed it very highly. It is like an apotheosis of the old school in the new era, a task for the well-intentioned *bravura* pianist.

When Liszt came to St. Petersburg, I, with both the Counts Wielhorski, accompanied him to Henselt's; we found the artist awaiting us and ready to comply with Liszt's particular request that he should play for him. Henselt gave us first *his own* reading of the Weber *Polacca in E*. I watched Liszt; his features expressed a certain astonishment. After Henselt had finished Liszt said: "I could have had velvet paws too, if I had wished!" (*"J'aurais pu me donner ces pattes de velours, si j'avais voulu!"*)

Liszt's approval was so unconditional that when —upon his second visit to St. Petersburg—I remarked that Henselt had made great progress, he replied: "Learn that an artist such as Henselt does not *make progress.*" (*"Apprenez, qu'un artiste, comme Henselt, ne fait pas des progrès."*) It was a reproof, —but it was a reproof from Liszt!

Great Piano Virtuosos

Henselt's execution of Weber's *Polacca* is a phenomenon. It is a union of the grandest power and strength with the greatest tenderness, in the interpretation of the poetic thought. With the very first measure (trill) under Henselt's hands, arises a vision of a brilliantly lighted Walhalla; kings walk there with fair women to whom they whisper words of love;—and then the Trio!—Henselt published his Variations to this inspiration of the knightly tone-poet, to this foremother of Polonaises, in St. Petersburg. There are not alone reinforcements; inner parts, more sonorous registers, *double* passages instead of mere *threads*, elevate the piece upon the shield of the Olympian present-day pianoforte, leaving to the original a certain feeling of *tonal emptiness*, which, in its time, was *fullness of tone*. But the thought, the creation, of Weber, still lives immortal!—What Henselt has woven into the work, it is like the journal of his soul, in the enjoyment of its intercourse with Weber! It is no improvement, no *editio emendatior*, but the homage of our modern piano — after fifty years of development — to its emancipator. One of Henselt's specialties is his interpretation of Weber, to whom, after all, he stands in closest human affinity. But Henselt discriminates

Adolph Henselt

in Weber. He discriminates between the value of the idea, and its often insufficient realization in the developments. Hans von Bülow is of the same mind; Tausig manifested the same in his arrangement of the *Invitation*; and Liszt has just published his arrangement of Weber's piano-compositions. At present Henselt is busy with an edition of his own reading of the solo sonatas—a reading which is the result of a lifetime of careful study, and not the passing fancy of a moment.

Of Weber's Piano-quartet and Trio (with flute); of the *Sonata in E minor* (the fourth); of the *Polacca* and the *Rondo in E flat*; of the two first Piano-concertos (in C, and E flat), and of the *Variations*, Henselt refuses to take any notice. On the other hand, he considers the Sonatas in C and A flat major, and in D minor, the Clarinet-sonata in E flat, the *Invitation* (his arrangement of which appeared early in St. Petersburg), the *Momento capriccioso*, the *Polacca in E*, and above all the *Concertstück*, the very highest expression of all piano-poetry. His interpretation of the *Concertstück* is extraordinary, and if we look at Weber from Henselt's standpoint it is unapproachable! Henselt throws his own life, his very soul and being into Weber; he does not

Great Piano Virtuosos

play Weber objectively, and probably no composer yields more readily to a subjective interpretation than Weber—whose work we understand as *redeeming the sensual through the ideal*. Weber is *love;* flirtations, French or other, are foreign to his nature!— If it were possible to lose Germany, we should find her again in *Der Freischütz!*— As Weber is in *Der Freischütz*, so is he in his piano-music. Weber is the last of the knights; he is the Ideal, ushered by the Artist into the prosy monotony of everyday life,—that image of Womanhood, which even the prosiest man of affairs, in the sackcloth and ashes of debit and credit, will not wave away!

Thus Henselt, his most faithful shield-bearer, interprets him. Henselt's most important interpretations of Weber are his *Polacca in E;* the *A flat major Sonata;* the *Rondo of the D minor Sonata*, where the episode in G (with the trills in the song-figure in the bass) is expressed in a manner which I had not believed among the possibilities of the piano — it always sounded to me like an unspeakably lovely spring song!—These interpretations of Weber culminated in the *Concertstück;* to hear Henselt play this is an event, the memory of which one carries

Adolph Henselt

through life! He gives it the happiest reading; it takes on quite a different appearance—it seems to prophesy the future of the piano as foreseen from the date of its composition, in the early twenties. And this subversion of all Hummel's ideas of pianoplaying was accomplished by a pupil of Hummel, *quantum mutatus ab illo!* In order to render the contrast between then and now still more striking —to give to the affair a still more fateful appearance than it bore at first glance—let us add, that Henselt has by no means ceased to be a good Hummel pupil; that the artist does his best by the well-known sonatas dedicated to Father Haydn, the *Fantasia in E flat* (Op. 18), the Quintet, and the Trios by Hummel; yet [24] these works, from Weber's height, are like the toys of childhood. Thus wonderfully is Henselt's nature divided between the doctrines of the good old school, and the acquisitions of the new!— He arranged the *Concertstück* to be played without accompaniment—that is, he so successfully altered the poem that one does not miss the orchestra, but is carried away with admiration of the composition. Of this, but one example. Before the entrance of the March *pp* (the return of the warrior— in the distance) where the

Great Piano Virtuosos

alluring magic of the bassoon-tone, and the hushed vibration of the stringed instruments *(tremolo pp)*, prepare for the *Marcia* which ranks alone in the history of music,—Henselt introduces *volate*, short but magnificent forerunners of the closing presto in six-eight, which are strikingly effective and quite in the spirit of the situation, for they foreshadow the *presto* figure—in which the lady of the castle joyfully embraces her returning lord.—Weber himself left us the programme of this piece (in the biography by his son).

Henselt's arrangements for two hands (one should have at least four to play them) are epoch-making in "arrangement"-literature: the three opera-overtures by Weber, several song-numbers from *Der Freischütz*, *Oberon*, and *Euryanthe* and the *Coriolanus Overture* by Beethoven. No orchestra would be able to render the *Oberon* overture with the fine *nuances*, with the flowingly blended euphony, with the intricate meaning, with which Henselt imbues this instrumental tale! Perfection of this kind is possible only to Unity in the Executant, not to any group of factors, despite the advantage of dissimilar tone-colors in the orchestra. This interpretation is, indeed, wholly incomparable.

Adolph Henselt

At rare, gracious moments, for his own enjoyment, Henselt plays the Weber operas four-handed; at these times it is easier to be his audience than his partner. His "Agathas" and "Ännchens" were better than any I ever heard on any other stage, and I have heard them all. What shall I say of *his* Gypsy choruses from *Preciosa?* Astounding; why Henselt never went to the theatre, became quite clear! That in Weber the artist is eclectic, is his right as a virtuoso; for others (and I think they have been the gainers thereby), the piano-quartets and trio, and the other compositions which Henselt rejected, have become life-long friends. Are not the *Sonates progressives et agréables* (in which only the French conventional title can be found fault with)—arranged for four hands from the too meagre original for piano and violin—operas in disguise? Is not everything comprehended within the bounds of Weber's original *Pièces* for four hands?

Henselt considers the Clarinet-sonata in E flat Weber's greatest work in respect of completeness and unity of design, and he arranged the charming piece for two pianos. On the second he gives the clarinet-part in his happy style of accompaniment—a style which no one else could attempt. By this means he obtains a unity and fullness of tone, and a general effect, by which the work gains in a high degree. The artist carries this second part in his heart—he never wrote it down. He also accompanied several of his great Études on a second piano, and in St. Petersburg he had a second part to the Cramer Études engraved. The artist considers the Études by Church-Father Cramer, which contrast so strongly with the Weber Muse, such great works of art, that he produces them in St. Petersburg, where his predilection is well known, on two pianos as full-fledged concert-pieces; and the *secondo* part so skillfully adapted to the *primo* (the unaltered original), that one can hardly believe they were ever played otherwise. To us these productions of Cramer's Études appear, viewed as repertory-pieces, like the comments of a philologist on a classic author. They are a culmen in the pedagogic fruit-garden; from an artistic standpoint, I never enjoyed them—*candidus imperti*. But how old Church-Father Cramer *(Beda venerabilis)* would have rejoiced to find himself so honored after a lapse of seventy years! How delicately and tastefully Henselt handled them; to invent a second part to the polyphonic compositions of Cramer—always so complete in themselves—is

Adolph Henselt

a problem for the connoisseur. It is a far greater achievement than that of Gounod, who composed a second part to the well-known Bach prelude. Think of the variety of form and rhythm, of expression and conception, contained in the Cramer Études! It was an *opus desparatum*; the thought of such a work could have occurred only to a German mind—and only the greatest love for the composition and the pleasure of solving such a difficult problem could have induced him to attempt it.

On several of the celebrated Moscheles Études (that in A flat, for instance), Henselt has also bestowed the blessing of the modern piano, and paid the greatest compliment to Moscheles by playing these variations to him in Leipzig. How astounded the neat little man must have been (we knew him very well) to see Henselt hurl his Achilles spear into the midst of his compositions!

The great German artist to whom this sketch is devoted despised ostentation and avoided publicity, yet he won renown in the German fatherland, and we believe these hints of his experiences in a foreign land will—to the German reader—form a welcome contribution to the history of the piano of our day.

The compass of a book is necessary for a detailed

description of such an important artist as Adolf Henselt.

Therefore we do not pretend to have exhausted our subject, and I can but assure the friendly reader that, to the best of our ability, we have endeavored to draw in outlines (as the English say) one of the most remarkable artistic phenomena of this century.

In closing, let us glance for a moment at the outward appearance of the artist—which is oftener mistaken for an exponent of the inner man, than one might think.

When Henselt first came to St. Petersburg, he was a perfect example of the German youth, of the Hun, the Germanic hero confident of success, without foreign polish. There was a suggestion of *Siegfried* in his character; one could read something of the Nibelungen in his deep, speaking eyes—young men and maidens have been intoxicated by reading the legend, both here and yonder! Throughout Germany one finds many portraits of the artist taken at this period. In one especially (which is taken full face) he looks you frankly in the eyes and you discern the romantic trait which is so prominent in his character—the never-satisfied soul continually striving to reach the ideal of absolute perfection.

Adolph Henselt

Henselt is an ego, a distinct personality. Like Liszt and Chopin, he is the fountain-head of a current, a tendency, on the pianoforte, and his own ancestor. It would be impossible to imitate Henselt's reproduction, because it is specifically individual; for this reason Henselt is without successors, and the best of his pupils in Russia, though true virtuosi, reproduce only his material side, not his heart, which remains his own, being inseparable from his total personality.

If any one ever approached Weber at the piano, it is Henselt; he, like Weber, is a spirit—a cosmos of ideas, such as one can find only in ages of the organic life of art. There can never be another Weber, for the reason that he lived at a time when people had leisure for contemplation and possessed greater power of thought and feeling than in our day: we find it difficult to believe that such a time ever existed!

It is not alone in his fruitful treatment of the piano that Henselt resembles Weber; it is not in the tenths and the chord-stretches, from which Henselt, like Weber, reaps advantage;—it is in the spirit, influencing the soul from the German soul, and not from speculative musical ideas; it is the life of the

Great Piano Virtuosos

German heart, which is sufficient unto itself, and courts nothing foreign; as the romantic poet has it:

> *Überwunden von der Schönheit,*
> *Will ich ewig nach dir ziehen.* *

Henselt's nature suggests an indestructible sense of youthfulness; such a nature cannot grow old, it must be and remain like itself alone. In Germany one sees among gray-haired statesmen a like youthfulness of thought; it is a legacy of the German academic life with them, but with our artist it is the German soul:—

> *—in dem die Welt sich,*
> *Die Ewige spiegelt!*

---

* *Kaiser Octavianus.*

Notes

Notes

Note 1

"*Des Leibes bist du ledig:
Gott sei der Seele gnädig.*"

Note 2

In Riga, since 1828, *Der Freischütz* had been a personality with whom all had social intercourse. The text was familiar language: "I have the Overture for four hands," caused peremptory invitations to evening entertainments. No barrel-organ but played "Und ob die Wolke sich verhülle;" no bowling-alley where the "Jägerchor" was not heard; no dance-hall that did not use the Waltzes; no bread-and-butter Miss who did not know "Jungfernkranz" and "veilchenblaue Seide;" no marriageable maiden who did not know "Kommt ein schlanker." The hunter, coming home with only two small snipe, excused himself with: "Alles was ich konnt' erschauen;" the husband, delayed by a glass of punch at the club, with: "Schwach war ich, obwohl kein Bösewicht."—"Doch hast du auch vergeben den Vorwurf, den Verdacht?" was the last question the wife asked, before going to sleep. Pigeons, long past all dangers of being shot at, employed an allegorical: "Schiess nicht, ich bin die Taube!" "Die süsse Stimme ruft," said the tenor, going to the duet at the piano; "konnt' ich das zu hoffen wagen?" sang every contented one. "Samiel hilf!" was an entertaining little society cry; "Bei den Pforten der Hölle," the confirmation of every promise; not a nail was hammered in without: "Schelm, halt' fest." Women, who in no wise doubted the possibility that even an unloaded gun might go off, stood their ground bravely for three shots in *Der Freischütz*. *Der Freischütz* travelled even into the country *(rus evolavit)*; every tree-trunk transformed itself at evening into the hunter "der im Dunkeln wacht." Such a union of all forces, all classes, all professions, as never before! All had a personal interest in Weber's music, and the rôles distributed as follows: every proprietor of an estate, was *Ottokar*, who led in the hunt; every forester was *Kuno;* every lover of the god Bacchus was *Kaspar;* each and every lover, with or without a gun, impersonated *Max;* the entire feminine population, were either *Ännchens* or *Agathes* without *tertium comparationis*. Such was our *Robin des bois!* How much of *that* could a Frenchman appreciate?

Note 3
Vien qua, Dorina bella; Thême russe; Thême original; and the Joseph Variations.

Note 4
See Lenz: *Beethoven et ses trois styles*, Sonata Op.

Notes

26, where I endeavored to give a sketch of this curious pianist.

Note 5
" Die, bird, or eat! " [Root, hog, or die!]

Note 6
Supremacy.

Note 7
The term *Lorette* is two or three centuries old; it has come into vogue latterly through Alphonse Karr. — *Translator's Note.*

Note 8
Valse mélancolique (A minor). In the eighth measure, highest part, occur the notes d (quarter) d $g\,sharp$ (quarter) over the first d; by taking $g\,sharp$ and c, but b to g and $d\,sharp$, a close results (one part). It has a fine effect to repeat the passage at the *reprise*.

Note 9
See Lenz: *Beethoven, eine Kunststudie*, Part iv, at Op. 95, p. 266.

Note 10
Compare, in this regard, Op. 10, No. 12; Op. 25, No. 7; Op. 34, No. 2; Op. 51; Op. 64, No. 3, in the Mazurkas,—among others, Op. 33, No. 4, B minor, where the left hand has an unaccompanied solo.

Note 11
See the *Signale for the Musical World* (1868, Nos. 37

to 39), wherein my musical conscience called upon me to take up the cudgels for Weber.

Note 12

Humor, a devotional, artistic wantonness, distinguishes the German from the Southron. Of this specific racial difference the *Times* once wrote: "The French have no humor. That poor, pitiful stuff of theirs, called *wit*, is nothing but thin, sour, blue-colored *claret*— a very different thing from the full, rich port-wine flavored growth, dear to Englishmen."

Note 13

In the *Neue freie Presse* of Sept. 1, 1871, in a supplement devoted to the Bonn celebration, Dr. Nohl collected, with praiseworthy zeal, some communications of Holz, the second violin of the Schuppanzigh Quartet, in the time of Beethoven, whose amanuensis he was, and to whom the master revealed much. I carried on a diligent correspondence with Holz; he copied for me, out of his musical diary, all the information Beethoven had given him relating to the last five quartets—and in these Holz had played the second violin and had, therefore, stood next the composer. These letters which Holz wrote me, being a valuable source of information, I turned over to the Imperial Public Library in St. Petersburg; but the contents are given word for word in the sixth volume of my book *Beethoven*,

Notes

eine Kunststudie in connection with Op. 127, the first of the five last quartets. It is the only information we possess relating to these Sybilline books, and we *know* that it is genuine.

I met Dr. Nohl at the Secular Festival at Vienna in December, 1870; he, Sérow, and I sat together at the concert, and Sérow told me—probably for the sake of saying something agreeable—that Dr. Nohl had told him that he had gotten most of his information about Beethoven from my book. Consequently, Dr. Nohl at least knows my book; it is astonishing that Holz, who gave me the information which is printed in my book, should also have given the same data to some one else, without once mentioning the fact to me. I was really but the medium, to preserve in a permanent form, the data obtained from Holz by Frau Fanny Lingbauer (*née* Tonsing), at that time living in Pesth. I had, for some years, carried on a correspondence with Frau Lingbauer, who was an enthusiastic connoisseur of Beethoven literature. It was not at all easy for this excellent lady to obtain from the kind-hearted Holz —who not only wrote badly, but expressed himself badly, too—these important facts relating to the last five quartets. I herewith offer Frau Lingbauer my renewed thanks. It was not decreed that I should become acquainted with my kind Beethoven correspon-

Great Piano Virtuosos

dent of Vienna and Pesth. My immature, but well-intentioned first book about Beethoven, published in the French language: *Beethoven et ses trois styles* (St. Petersburg, 1852, *Bernard*, 2 vols.; two pirated editions—*Stapleaux*, Brussels, 1854; *Lavinée*, Paris, 1855), was in such demand in 1852, that through the Austrian Embassy in St. Petersburg I received from Frau Lingbauer a Beethoven trophy—one of those ingeniously photographed groups of Beethoven relics, consisting of the best bust of Beethoven, his Lichnowski violin and the lithograph of the master at work upon his *Missa Solemnis*, an autograph from the last quartets, and a portrait of our good Holz. This photograph of the Beethoven relics, so often copied, was one of two original large quarto photographs, and I presented it to the library of the Imperial Hofsängerkapelle in St. Petersburg. As to the data of Dr. Nohl which appeared in the *Neue freie Presse*, I may say: *first*,—that we ought at last to leave off writing—according to Schindler and Holz—"l'œuvre *le* plus accom*pli*," as Beethoven called the *Mass in D* in a letter to Cherubini, since it should be called "*la* plus accom*plie* ;" and here there is no reason for the diplomatic conservation of a grammatical error. *Secondly*,—the *Tenth Symphony* was not, as Dr. Nohl said, in C minor; it was sketched in E flat major (the *Scherzo* in C minor and C major). Holz sent me a copy of the

Notes

sketches for it, and since the beginning of the world there has not been a greater intellectual loss to deplore than that of the *Tenth Symphony. Thirdly,*—the slow middle movement in the *F minor Quartet* is no extraordinary *Adagio*, as Dr. Nohl writes, but an extraordinary *Allegretto (ma non troppo)*, and this sign of Beethoven's is specific, and important to the proper reading of the composition. That which Dr. Nohl says further on: "At night, when the heavens were alight with millions of stars, Beethoven walked across the fields at Baden; his glance swept questioningly and longingly into endless space"—is more important and significant than anything which has hitherto appeared about the immortal quartets; and these communications of Dr. Nohl are, altogether, of high value. But, in comparison to Beethoven's own utterances, we all—who have labored with endless toil in these spheres—are but as dust!

Note 14
The title of a satirical publication printed in Berlin.

Note 15
Meyerbeer said: "Can one reduce women to notation? They would breed mischief, were they emancipated from the measure!"—See No. 37 of the *Neue Berliner Musik-Zeitung*, 1871 ("Berliner Bekannstschaften").

Great Piano Virtuosos

Note 16
A fact which I think I was the first to point out (in *Beethoven, eine Kunststudie*, vol. iii., p. 152, touching Op. 15).

Note 17
A Russian coin, value about 77 cents.

Note 18
See *Beethoven, eine Kunststudie*, Part 4, pp. 159 *et seq.;* an entire little monograph—yet not so much, after all!—

> "*In seiner Werkstatt träume sich der Künstler*
> *Zum Bildner einer schönern Welt!*"

Note 19
Schiller: "*Was die Mode streng getheilt.*"

Note 20
These essays were written about 1868.—*Translator's Note.*

Note 21
For a proper appreciation of Henselt's triumph, and of the peculiar situation in St. Petersburg, it must be observed, that for thirty years Charles Mayer had held the first place in St. Petersburg, and did not lack supporters, and yet was never able to play even once before the Court (the height of his ambition); he finally left St. Petersburg and went to Dresden, where he died.

Notes

Note 22

The chord referred to is only the well-known horn-passage in the *Eroica*, strengthened by the greatest conceivable dissonance; in other words, it is a *cumulus* of dominant and tonic, motivated by the idea with which Beethoven was filled. The opinion of my dear friend, C. F. Weitzmann of Berlin, I cannot agree with. He thinks that the chord is not an independent one, but a pedal-point figure like all chords, built up of successive thirds, which overstep the limits of an octave. See the Justification of the Chord by the *Idea*, in *Beethoven, eine Kunststudie*, Lenz, vol. vi., page 194.

Note 23

French Civilization and German Humanism from the book lately published in Berlin—a book full of instruction and of deep thought: "*Vaterländische Erinnerungen und Betrachtungen über den Krieg von 1870–1871.*"